CHILDREN'S ENCYCLOPEDIA

DISCOVER YOUR WORLD

STERLING

CONTENTS

INTRODUCTION

TRIPS, SCIENCE, AND TECHNOLOGY

Since ancient times, people have travelled to obtain food and natural resources, to sell and buy goods, or conquer new territories. This is how we have learned about other ways of thinking and understanding the world that have formed the foundations of science and technology today. In this book we offer you a trip trough science and technology, a trip through time from now to antiquity, and also through different corners of the earth and the immensity of the universe.

TO BEGIN

In each chapter we will begin speaking of a type of trip and we will indicate the centuries in which it took place and also what discoveries were made during that time.

INTERVIEWS WITH THE MAIN CHARACTERS

We have made an imaginary trip through time in order to interview Some of the most curious people from the history of science and technology.

EXPERIMENT AND OBSERVE

With the experiments you will have the opportunity to play with making science and developing technologies.

A GAME FOR YOU!

With this game you will enjoy learning much of the information and curiosities of the book. Here you will play with counters with the main characters of science, with a dice you make yourself, with 72 questions and answers, and with a board to get you to the finishing line.

THE TRIPS TO SPACE

20TH CENTURY – 21ST CENTURY

To know the Universe better we have done a lot of investigations and have developed very innovative technologies. You will learn to make a homemade rocket, the destiny of the Universe and discover the consequences of famous theories.

The conquest of space has changed our way of seeing the world, whose borders extend to the infinity of the Universe. The great projects of investigation have attained surprising results and the discoveries have not only added to our knowledge, but also improved the technology of war.

THE EARTH IS BLUE
(Yuri Gagarin)
During the Soviet mission Vostok, Yuri Gagarin was the first person who saw our planet from outside and was surprised to see that it is so blue.

Ready, set...GO!
The participants in the Space Race were the old Soviet Union and the United States of America. Both competed fiercely to demonstrate to the entire world who was more powerful. The USSR won points with the first satellite and the first human being in space, but the U.S. had two astronauts land on the Moon.

The Earth: A Special Planet

Of all the planets that make up the solar system, the Earth is the only one that supports life. This is a planet where the surface temperatures remain moderate because of the presence of water and an atmosphere. The crust remains very active geologically and is in a continual state of formation.

Life as we know it can survive only on planets where there is water in liquid form. The atmosphere acts like a protective shield against lethal radiation and meteorites.

The Unseen Side

The first images of the far side of the Moon were obtained in 1959, thanks to the photographs sent back to Earth by the Soviet space probe, Luna 3.

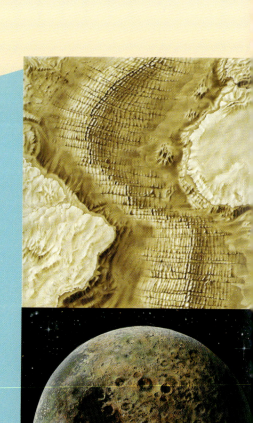

Day or Night?

In the areas near the Earth's Poles, there are several months when there is only night, and others when it's always day. This is due to the angle of inclination of the Earth's rotational axis.

Always the Same Side

Since the Moon takes the same amount of time to complete a revolution on its axis as a complete rotation around the Earth, the same side always faces our planet.

One of the largest impact craters on Moon is the South Pole. Aitleen Basin that is roughly 2,500 km in diameter.

The best time to observe the lunar relief with binoculars or a small telescope is in the waxing or appearing and waning or disappearing phases.

Tranquility

The first astronauts on the Moon walked in the Sea of Tranquility.

Did you know that...

The Moon experiences earthquakes that are detectable from the Earth.

Collision Course!

Halley's Comet, which came close to the Earth in 1986, experienced a collision with some celestial body in 1993 that made it increase in size. When it next approaches the Earth, in 2062, we will be able to see the effects of the collision.

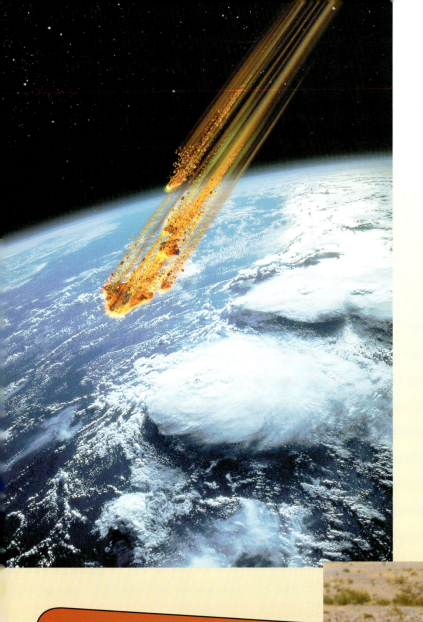

Robots ON MARS

In order to obtain samples of rocks and images of Mars or the Moon, remote control vehicles called "Rovers", were used.

Travelling rocks

The meteorites are made of particles of dust, ice, and rock that arrive to the surface of a planet and form a crater. They bring with them much valuable information about the solar system. Their origin could be due to asteroids and comets.

The shooting stars that we see on some nights are actually meteorites that burn when they enter the earth's atmosphere.

GRAVITY AS FUEL

In order for the space missions to last many years and move through space without fuel, they use the force of gravity.

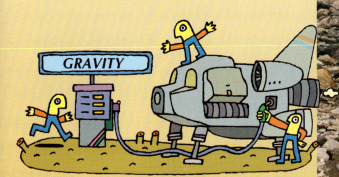

GRAVITY

TO SHOW CENTRIFUGAL FORCE

Procedure

1. Tie the stone to the rubber band.
2. Whirl the stone around in a circle at arm's length. Can you see the tension in the rubber? This is caused by a force acting on the stone directly outwards from the centre of the circle. It is called the centrifugal force. Centrifugal forces come into play whenever an object is moving in a circle.
3. Whirl the stone faster. The stretch on the rubber will increase because the centrifugal force increases with the speed of rotation.
4. While rotating, suddenly let go of the band. In which direction does the stone fly off?
5. A centrifugal force occurs because a rotating object wants to keep moving in a straight line but is pulled around in a circle. This is why the stone speeds off in a straight line as soon as it is released.

Where are Stars Born?

Nebulae are the raw materials from which stars were formed; their colors vary with their temperature.

Did you know that...
On December 27, 1872 there occurred the greatest shower of falling stars known, when the Earth passed through the tail of the broken-up comet Biela.

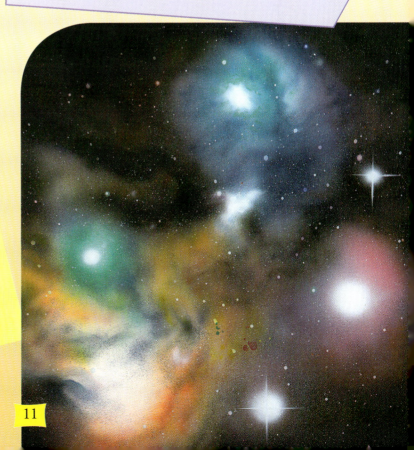

Outward Force...

Earth experiences a centrfugal force! It is an outword force and depends upon the object's mass, speed and distance. So, when the Sun pulls Earth towards it due to gravity, it prevents Earth from going in a straight line.

The Colours of Stars...

Colour	Temperature	Examples
Blue	25,000 - 11,000 K	Sirius, Vega, Rigel
Blue to White	7,000 - 6,000 K	Canopus
White to Yellow	6,000 - 5,000 K	Sun, Capella
Orange to Red	5,000 - 3,500 K	Arcturus
Red	below 3,500 K	Betelgeuse, Antares

THE BAND OF MILK

Among the many galaxies that make up the Universe, the one we know best is the Milky Way, since that is where we are located. Earlier, it was thought that a Goddess has spilled milk. Hence the name!

Count the Stars!

On a Moonless night and away from cities and other population centers, about 3,000 stars are visible to the naked eye.

The Milky Way contains around 300,000 stars.

DEATH SCREAMS

If a young star keeps up its irregular contractions for very long, it uses up all its fuel and dies after just a few million years. On the other hand, small stars are not as hot as large ones, so they "burn" more slowly and last longer.

BLACK HOLES

There are regions in the space from which nothing, even light, cannot escape. These are the black holes. They can't be seen, but its effects are visible.

The mass of a black hole is several times greater than that of the Sun, but it is only a few miles/kilometres in diameter.

THE WRATH OF GOD...

In ancient times, eclipses often were omens of evil occurrences, for it was supposed that the disappearance of the light was a punishment from the Gods. Today, we understand that they are a phenomenon that is a product of the celestial workings obscuring or blocking the light and casting shadows on each other.

ATTENTION!

You must never observe a solar eclipse directly, as it can cause serious damage to the eyes. You have to use special glasses.

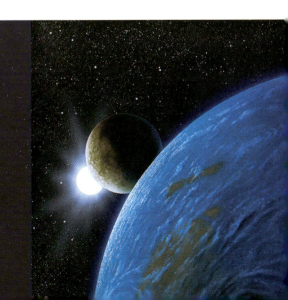

13

COPERNICUS, KEPLER, AND GALILEO

During the sixteenth century these three astronomers did the basic work that completely transformed the concept of the Universe. After many calculations and observations, Copernicus declared that the Earth was not the centre of the Universe, Galileo demonstrated that Copernicus was right and conducted observations with the help of the telescope that he had invented.

India

Indian mathematicians created the concept of zero, a concept that took many centuries to take root in the human mind.

Babylonia

As early as 5,000 years ago the inhabitants of Babylon (modern-day Iraq), recorded on their tables the regularity of certain celestial phenomena, such as the changes in the phases of the Moon and the movement of the Sun.

China

Three thousand years ago, the Chinese constructed astronomical observatories that divided the year into four seasons.

The Chaldeans invented the water clock to measure time in their observations.

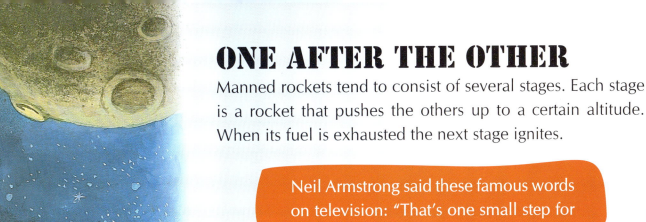

ONE AFTER THE OTHER

Manned rockets tend to consist of several stages. Each stage is a rocket that pushes the others up to a certain altitude. When its fuel is exhausted the next stage ignites.

Neil Armstrong said these famous words on television: "That's one small step for [a] man, one giant leap for mankind."

Many had feared that the surface of the Moon was made of dust and that any spacecraft that landed would immediately sink. Experience showed otherwise.

SIX TIMES ON THE MOON
There have been six other manned expeditions to the Moon (Apollo 12 to Apollo 17) since the first landing.

Skylab, the first American space station was put into orbit in 1973; as a result it became possible for teams of astronauts to stay in space for several months.

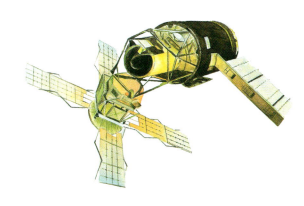

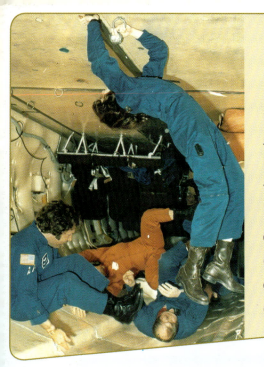

ZERO GRAVITY

During the launch of a spaceship, the human body weighs up to ten times more than normal. Weightlessness, the absence of gravity, causes decalcification of the bones after an extended period of time.

Muscular Weakness

Astronauts who remain in space for several months suffer from muscular weakness because of the lack of gravity, and when they return to Earth, they have to be carried on a stretcher until they regain their strength.

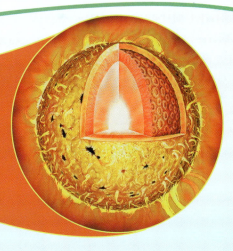

Sol or Helios or The Sun?

The Romans Called the Sun as Sol, while the Greeks named it Helios. The Sun is a modest star located in a corner of our galaxy, Still, we depend on it to live, and because it is so close, we know it better than any other star.

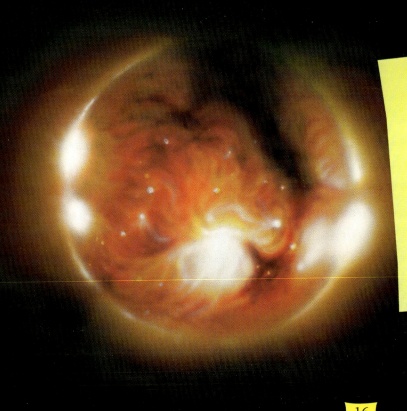

Did you know that...

- The diameter of the Sun is around 100 times greater than that of the Earth
- The Sun weighs around 330,000 times more than the Earth.
- In producing energy, the Sun consumes 600 million tonnes of hydrogen every second.

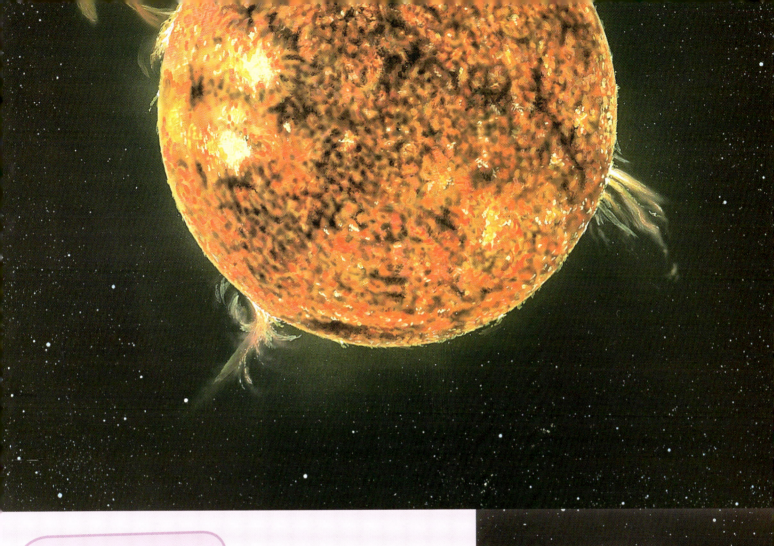

The most recent period of maximum solar activity was in 2008.

The greatest solar prominences that cause interference on Earth that affects telecommunications.

Solar prominences in the form of a loop (quiescent prominences) don't achieve much height, but can last for months!

TEMPERATURE

Sunspots are around 7,200°F (4,000°C).

The End of the Earth

When the Sun has consumed all its hydrogen and helium reserves, it will turn into a Red Giant; it will then increase considerably in size. The nearest planets such as Mercury and Venus will be engulfed and the heat will be so intense on our planet that every form of life will disappear.

Depending on the Sun

Since the Sun has adequate reserves for another five billion years, our planet still has that much time to live.

2012: Doomsday!
Predictions had been made as early as the Mayans, that the world will end in the year 2012. Claims had been made that a fictitious planet, Nibiru, would collide with Earth. But according to NASA, these are all fake. Phew, what a scare!!

THE DWARF

Pluto was the ninth planet of the solar system, but since 2006 it is considered a Dwarf.

M-V-E-M-J-S-U-N

The mnemonic, which is a learning technique, for the eight planets is: "My Very Educated Mother Just Served Us Nachos".

THE EXPERIMENT

SPACE ROCKET

1. Pass the rope inside the two little pieces of straw and tie an end in a high place. Ask an adult for help so that your rocket can get very high.

2. Inflate your balloon, close the mouthpiece with the clothes pin and glue together the two pieces of straw with the tape, one in every end of the balloon so that the mouthpiece faces down. You can also decorate your space ship with a permanent felt-tip pen.

3. Tie the other end of the rope to an object on the floor, for example a leg of a chair.

4. Hold the clothes pin from below. Now you can start the countdown: 10, 9, 8, 7, 6, 5, 4, 3, 2, 1... zero! Press and open the clothes pin and release your space ship

Observe your spaceship: Why does it rise rapidly? It's because of the loss of air inside. The real spaceships get to leave the Earth's atmosphere because they rapidly lose the gases from the combustion process.

3 2 1 ZERO!!!,

19

MOONS OF METAL

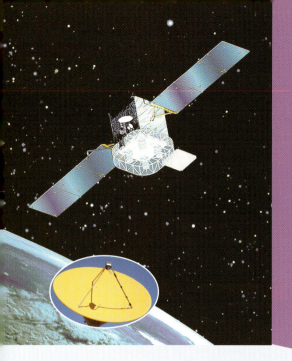

The artificial satellites are like the Moon: they move around the planet. They can turn around the Earth or other celestial bodies. They obtain information and afterwards they send it to the Earth in the form of waves.

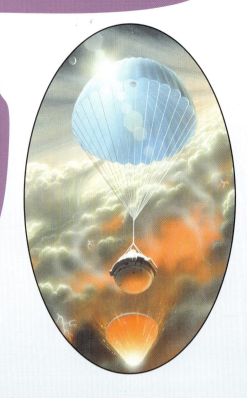

From space to home

Many objects that surround us have been invented to be used in space like barcodes, the joysticks of videogames, plasma televisions and teflon skillets.

PARACHUTE MACHINES

The space probes have parachutes so that the instruments of measurement and analysis of rocks, gases, and others do not break when they separate from the spaceship.

Floating laboratories

The space stations are laboratories where astronauts study the Universe and where they spend time working.

No plugs among the stars

The energy used in stations and space probes comes from photovoltaic power stations.

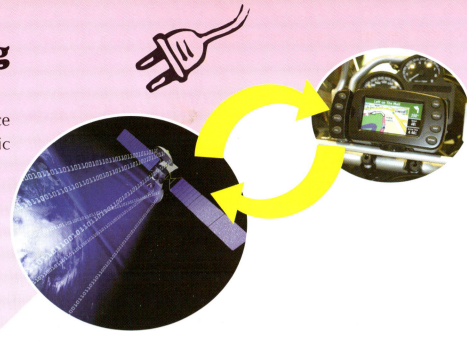

Turn to the left

The GPS equipment that indicates directions receives information from positioning satellites that rotate around the Earth at its same speed.

MATERIAL:

- A glass bottle that is empty and transparent
- Cork
- Cotton thread
- Screw
- Magnifying glass

EXPERIMENT:

The energy of the Sun

1. Tie the screw at one end of the thread and hang it from the neck of the bottle.
2. Put the cork in the bottle.
3. Place the bottle under the Sun and, using a magnifying glass, direct the Sun beams to a point on the thread.

After a while you will see how the thread burns and breaks. Notice how the magnifying glass concentrates the solar energy. This is why you should never look into the Sun through a magnifying glass because this would hurt your vision.

WHAT DO YOU WANT TO BE WHEN YOU ARE OLDER:
ASTRONAUT, COSMONAUT, OR TAIKONAUT?

If someone asks you this question you can answer any of the three words, as they all refer to the same profession. If you are European or from the United States you will say that you want to be an astronaut, if you are Russian, a cosmonaut, and if you are Chinese, a taikonaut.

DROUGHT IN SPACE

There is no way of obtaining water in space, therefore the astronauts do not shower. They wash themselves with humidity towels and in the space stations they recycle the water from air and from urine.

Valentina Tereshkova
In 1963, she became the first woman astronaut and broke the record of longest stay in space.

If you want to grow, go to space

Because in space there is no gravity, the spinal column stretches, that's why the astronauts return taller, although afterwards they go back to their normal height.

IMAGINARY INTERVIEW WITH

LAIKA
(?-1957)

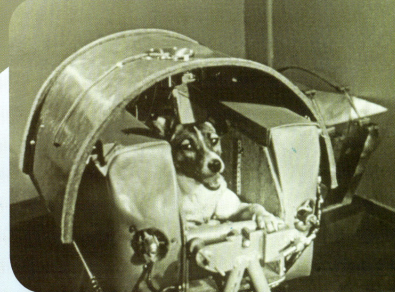

— *Dear Laika, when wandering through the streets of Moscow did you ever imagine that you would be famous for being the first animal astronaut of history?*

— Woof! What a question! The truth is that I used to look up to the sky and hope that someone would give me something to eat. I never imagined that I would fly in Sputnik 2.

— *Did your life change when you entered the Soviet space program?*

— Woof! It changed completely, I ate everyday and various times, and in exchange I had to train very hard. They put me in a kind of ship, very very small, and I experienced vibrations, noise, and accelerations.

— *And how was the experience of orbital flight?*

— I will tell you in one word: Wooffffffff! It was impressive. At first I was very scared, my heart beating a mile a minute. Afterwards I loved being without gravity, and I even looked down and I wanted to play with the blue ball that I saw, what you call Earth. But as travelling makes me hungry, I ate.

— *And to finish, what do you think about the circumstances of your death not being clarified until 2002?*

— You know, it was all politics, for those were the times of the Cold War. If my bosses communicated that I had died after 7 hours they would have lost points in the Space race. What's more, to admit that they could not grant my trip back to Earth would have given them a bad image of being cruel.

CHARACTERISTICS OF MERCURY	
Median Distance from Sun	35,319,000 miles / 57,900,000 km
Mass	.055 times that of the Earth
Diameter	3,032 miles / 4,878 km
Length of Day	58 Earth days
Length of Year	88 Earth days
Surface Temperature Ranges	950° F day and −346° F night

A spaceship needs a speed of 2.6 miles per second to blast off from Mercury's surface.

Gravity on the surface of Mercury is .39 times that of Earth.

Mercury has a very weak magnetic field. It appears that there are vestiges of ice in the polar regions of the planet, but no one credits the possibility that it harbors any life.

CHARACTERISTICS OF VENUS	
Median Distance from Sun	65,880,000 miles / 108,000,000 km
Mass	0.81 times that of the Earth
Diameter	7,519 miles / 12,102 km
Length of Day	243 Earth days
Length of Year	225 Earth days
Surface Temperature	866° F/480° C

The clouds on Venus move at high speed, producing huge storms at that altitude.

Winds on the surface of the planet are mild, and since there are no clouds, the tops of the mountains are easily visible.

There are active volcanoes on Venus.

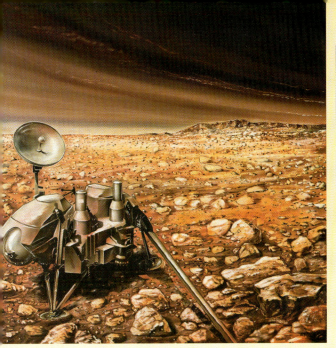

CHARACTERISTICS OF MARS	
Median Distance from Sun	139,000,000 miles / 228,000,000 km
Mass	.107 times that of the Earth
Diameter	4,139 miles / 6,786 km
Length of Day	24.5. hours
Length of Year	1.88 Earth years
Surface Temperature Ranges	from 68° F / − 220° F

Gravity on the surface of Mars is .38 times that of Earth; the speed a rocket needs to reach to escape from its surface is 3 miles (5 km)/sec.

The ice of the polar caps is made up of water and carbon dioxide; the latter is also the main component of the planet's thin atmosphere.

Strong dust storms are responsible for surface erosion on Mars.

It is believed that most of the water that exists on Mars is frozen in the subsoil.

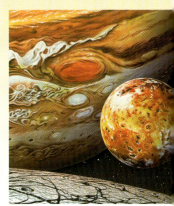

CHARACTERISTICS OF JUPITER	
Median Distance from Sun	474,580,000 miles / 778,000,000 km
Mass	318 times that of the Earth
Diameter	87,218 miles / 142,980 km
Length of Day	10 hours
Length of Year	11.9 Earth years
Surface Temperature	− 166° F / − 110° C

Jupiter is the largest planet in our solar system. It is a gas giant and the third brightest object in the sky.

- Gravity on the surface of Jupiter is 2.34 times that of Earth.
- The rocky core inside the planet makes up just 4 percent of its total mass.
- Jupiter gives off radio waves that can be detected with a home radio receiver on the frequency modulation band.

CHARACTERISTICS OF SATURN	
Median Distance from Sun	872,300,000 miles / 1,430,000,000 km
Mass	95.2 times that of the Earth
Diameter	73,529 miles / 120,540 km
Length of Day	10.5 hours
Length of Year	29.5 years
Surface Temperature	−240° F / −150° C

The Moon of Saturn, Mimas, measures 239 miles (392 km) in diameter and has a tremendous crater 61 miles (100 km) in diameter.

It appears that Saturn's rings are matter from a satellite that never formed.

The space probe Voyager has proven that the rings are really a series of many thin rings that are superposed on top of one another.

CHARACTERISTICS OF URANUS	
Median Distance from Sun	1,750,000 miles / 2,870,000,000 km
Mass	14.6 times that of the Earth
Diameter	31,182 miles / 51,118km
Length of Day	17.2hours
Length of Year	84 Earth years
Surface Temperature	−357°F / −216°C

Uranus is another of the giant planets, but given its distance from the Earth, it is scarcely visible with the naked eye. It has the same composition as the other gaseous planets, and it too rotates rapidly on its axis.

It also has several thin rings that are invisible through telescopes. It has 17 Moons (including five main ones) that have so far been discovered.

♀ Venus   ♂ Uranus   ♄ Saturn   ☿ Mercury

⊕ Earth   ♂ Mars   ♃ Jupiter   ♆ Neptune

CHARACTERISTICS OF NEPTUNE	
Median Distance from Sun	2,745,000,000 miles / 4,500,000,000 km
Mass	17.23 times that of the Earth
Diameter	30,212 miles / 49,528 km
Length of Day	16 hours
Length of Year	165 Earth years
Surface Temperature	−357° F / −216° C

Neptune is a blue gaseous planet that can be seen only with the aid of powerful binoculars. It has a very active atmosphere, as indicated by its spots and transverse bands. It is surrounded by a small ring and has eight Moons.

Nereida's diameter is 207 miles (340 km). It probably was a celestial body that was captured by the gravitational pull of Neptune.

Polar Auroras

This phenomenon is one of the most impressive ones caused by the arrival of charged particles in the Earth's atmosphere. However, the aurora can be observed only near the Polar Regions. The auroras take place when solar wind reaches the Earth's atmosphere and the electrons and protons emit beautifully coloured lights.

Did you know that...

Neptune's biggest Moon, Triton, measures 1,647 miles (2,700 km) in diameter and rotates in a direction opposite that of Neptune; as a result, its speed is gradually diminishing, and within a hundred million years it will fall into the planet and disappear.

A WONDERFUL SPECTACLE

For an observer on the ground, the polar auroras appear to be huge curtains of beautiful, coloured lights that move in the sky.

From space, the polar aurora looks like a circle of light around the pole.

Van Allen's Belts are areas that retain particles of solar wind due to the Earth's magnetic field.

CO-OPERATION FOR FINDING EXTRATERRESTRIALS

There is a project to search for intelligent extraterrestrial life that, in order to analyse extraterrestrial radio signals, uses the computers of volunteers from all over the world.

MESSAGE in a space bottle

In the same way that we launch bottles into the sea with messages, various space missions take messages for the possible beings that live on other planets that they might find. These messages have images of Earth, music, greetings in various languages, human figures, star maps, the double helix of DNA, etc.

VACATIONS TO THE MOON!

There are no flights offered to the Moon yet, but it is possible to travel to the International Space Station. But if you want to go, you need to undergo some medical tests and hard training, and also pay 20 million dollars.

The neutron stars were detected for the first time by Jocelyn Bell.

A SPACE TOURIST

In April, 2001, an American multimillionaire, Dennis Tito, became the first space tourist.

A BASE ON THE MOON?

The desire to colonize other heavenly bodies will probably begin with the Moon. The second planet to be colonized will probably be Mars, which offers similar conditions for constructing bases.

SHORTCUT THROUGH SPACE!

What if we could travel through time? Well, scientists are looking for a way through wormholes. If this can be achieved, perhaps the course of physics can be revised.

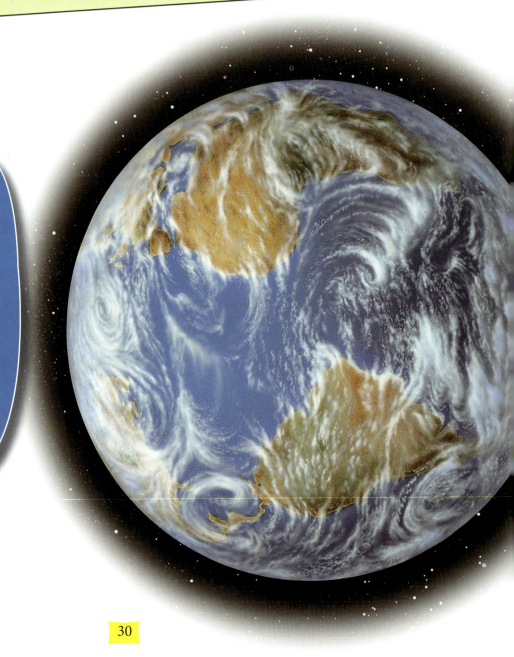

30

SPACE takes up a lot of SPACE!

Multiple space stations around the Earth, like the International Space Station (ISS), will be the first step in interplanetary travel; they will probably use the Moon as a launching site.

Interstellar distances are so astronomical - it is difficult to measure its expanse. If the Voyager space probe travels at 37,000 miles per hours, it will take 80,000 years to reach Proxima Century our nearest star (4.2 light years away).

$$E=mc^2$$

E=energy

m = mass

c = speed of light

—Mr. Einstein, why did the Times magazine call you the "person of the century"?

— I imagine it was because my two theories were a revolution in classical physics: the special theory of relativity and the general theory of relativity.

— But, there is something I don't understand. Why did they give you a Nobel Prize for your work about the photoelectric effect and not for those other theories?

—Things of science; at that time many scientists did not accept my ideas and it also seemed that some of them didn't even understand them.

— Do you know what your famous formula $E=mc^2$ was used for afterwards, besides appearing in all kinds of publicity?

— This formula set the foundation for the formation of nuclear energy and also has helped in great advances in astronomy.

— Are you a pacifist?

— I know why you ask me that question. I was a pacifist during the First World War, but I admit I supported the Manhattan project for developing the first atomic bomb.

— And what is so special about the general theory of relativity?

— It changes Newton's conception of gravity. Thanks to this theory we could calculate the orbit of Mercury and also find out that the light of the stars is curved.

Thank you very much and see you soon.

"IMAGINATION
IS MORE
IMPORTANT
THAN
KNOWLEDGE"

-ALBERT EINSTEIN

BIG BANG!

These very powerful words are the name of the theory that explains the origins of the Universe. According to this theory, everything began with a great explosion and afterwards the Universe has been expanding until our time.

EXPERIMENT

THE EXPANSION OF THE UNIVERSE OR THE

BIG CRUNCH

Material:
- A big balloon
- A permanent marker

1. Inflate your balloon a little bit.
2. Paint several galaxies with different forms and spread them out evenly.
3. Now inflate your balloon little by little.

Notice what happens with the galaxies of your balloon. Each time they separate more and in every direction. This is what would happen to the Universe according to the theory of the constant Expansion. But if you deflate the balloon at once, you will see what would happen according to the theory of the Big Crunch.

CLASSIFICATION OF THE GALAXIES:
- Elliptical and lenticular
- Spiral
- Spiral barred
- Irregular

SUBMARINES AND SCIENTIFIC REVOLUTIONS

The development of military submarine technology allowed us to better understand the bottom of the ocean, to notice that it is expanding, and to confirm that the continents are separating, just as the theory of the Continental Drift predicted. From this developed the theory of the Tectonic Plates that revolutionised our understanding of the volcanoes, the earthquakes, the formation of the mountains, etc.

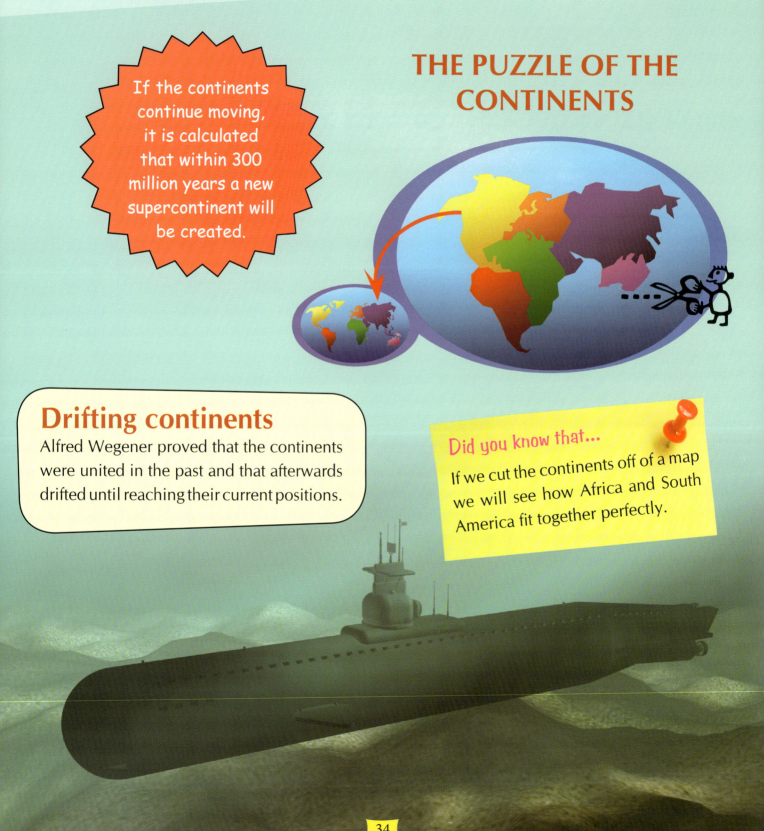

If the continents continue moving, it is calculated that within 300 million years a new supercontinent will be created.

THE PUZZLE OF THE CONTINENTS

Drifting continents

Alfred Wegener proved that the continents were united in the past and that afterwards drifted until reaching their current positions.

Did you know that...

If we cut the continents off of a map we will see how Africa and South America fit together perfectly.

Centre of the Universe

There is no centre or edge of the universe. We do not know whether the universe is finite or infinite!

Is the Earth Expanding?

Of course not, neither is the Milky Way. However, the distances between the clusters of galaxies are increasing. But, there is no limit to how fast the space can expand.

THE GREAT EXPLOSION

Did you know that...
The Universe is 14 billion years old. Time was created in the Big Bang, before that, time did not exist.

From the instant of the initial explosion the temperature of the Universe has been decreasing; that is also true of the speed at which it is expanding.

IS IT POSSIBLE...

Some theories suggest that our Universe is part of an infinity of Universes (Multiverses). This is possible but extremely difficult to prove.

THE FIRST ATOMS...

Three hundred thousand years after the Big Bang, the universe cooled off enough for the first atoms to be formed.

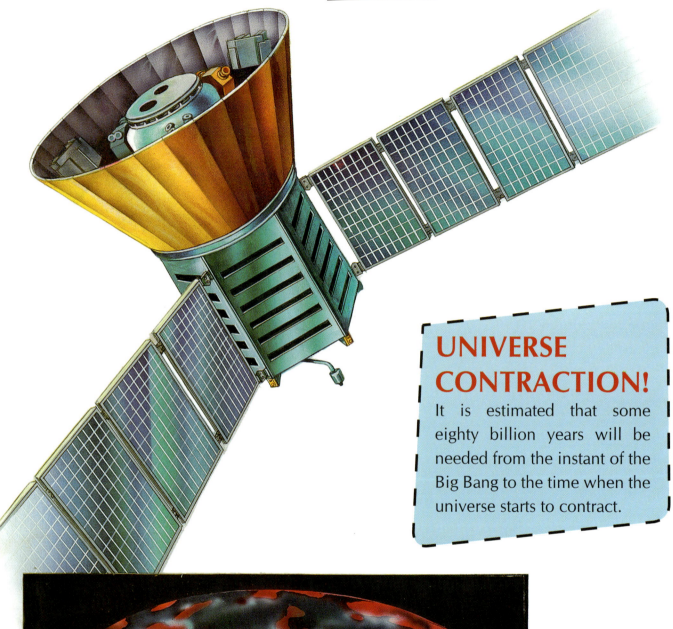

UNIVERSE CONTRACTION!

It is estimated that some eighty billion years will be needed from the instant of the Big Bang to the time when the universe starts to contract.

AS REAL AS ACTUAL LIFE... OR NOT?

Virtual reality (VR) is the representation of things across mediums of information and electronics. It gives you a sensation of movement, touch, images and sounds that seem real and it even allows you to interact with what surrounds you.

Where are we going?

BY 2029, 99% OF THE WORLD'S COMPUTING CAPACITY WILL BE NON-HUMAN.

Instantaneous interactions

In order for it to be virtual reality the interaction has to be instantaneous, in real time. It doesn't count if we touch something and it moves after three seconds. It must be immediate.

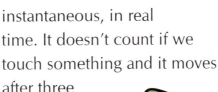

20 quadrillion calculations per second!

VR = HUMAN BRAIN SUPERCOMPUTERS

VIRTUAL VACATIONS

Confusing a virtual environment with a real place still seems unlikely. But judging by the speed of research, maybe when you are older you could bathe in a virtual beach without getting wet and ski without snow.

THE TOOLS

To perceive virtual reality we need a tool that provides a sensation: a helmet, a pair of gloves or even a mouse. In other words, we need an interface that makes us see, touch, hear or even makes us move.

FOR PLAYING AND FOR LEARNING

Virtual reality can be used for playing or for visiting museums, but also it has many scientific and industrial uses, like testing the comfort of a car, learning to make a surgical operation or building a space satellite.

THE TRIP TO INFORMATION

19TH CENTURY – 21ST CENTURY

The information technologies have changed our way of knowing the world. You will see how the information travels in the media, in cells, and in the brain, be able to build your own telephone and listen to the heartbeats of your friends.

38

THE TRIPS TO INFORMATION

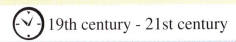

Information travels everywhere and in many ways: e-mail, the press, the radio, the television, the telephone, Internet and even through cells. Since the 19th century we have developed technologies of information that have increased the circulation of knowledge. The most recent is the Internet that also facilitates the development of collective knowledge.

The works of knowledge should be free, there is no reason it shouldn't be like this.
Richard Stallman

Send it to me by e-mail
One of the fastest ways for sending information is by Internet, using electronic mail commonly known as "e-mail".

WWW...
The web is an Internet service that allows you to access and spread digital information in the form of text, images and videos.

Everyone's together
Engineers, scientists, and fans of computer science collaborate on the development of free software that any person can use, modify, improve, copy, and spread for the benefit of humanity.

The first computer, which was named the Mark I, needed millions of feet of wiring to function, and it was not programmable; in other words, it could perform only the function for which it was built. With the introduction of the transistor, the computers of the 1960s became faster and much smaller, and were the source of today's personal computers.

FROM THE MARK I TO THE PC

The first computer that was totally electromechanical was developed for IBM by the American Howard Aiken between 1939 and 1944.

Home and office calculators are small computers that have a great capacity for performing calculations.

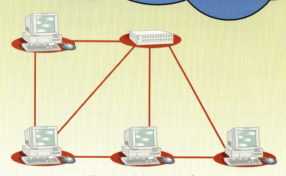

Tree Network

Bus Network

Ring Network

THE NET OF NETWORKS

Personal computers can be linked together to form networks and share information. This method of working has been especially useful in medium-sized businesses in a period of growth.

FULL THROTTLE AHEAD...

The Internet has developed only a part of its potential. When the financial, commercial, and technical problems inherent to anything so innovative are solved, it will be possible to realise the tremendous advantages that such a powerful medium for accessing information represents.

Communications and Electromagnetism

The development of the theories about electromagnetism led to the invention of various gadgets for communicating in the distance like the telephone, the radio, or the television.

89.3 FM

The great advances of the radio are based on the possibility of transmitting information at great distances without needing a cable. Instead, with a radio you need a system of emission and reception of electromagnetic waves.

The first emissions used the AM (amplitude modulation) until they invented the FM (frequency modulation), which improved the quality of sound.

PRESS

Technical advances have improved the written press, such as the invention of the printing press, offset printing, or digital printing.

cyan

magenta

yellow

black

four colour

FOUR COLOURS - CMYK!

Today, in colour printing four different plates are printed separately and used for black, yellow, cyan, and magenta. The mixing of these colours in different proportions produces all other colors.

Did you know that...

One of the most commonly used printing processes is offset, in which the ink that coats the metal plate is transferred to a sheet of rubber rolled onto a cylinder, which in turn transfers it to the paper.

PRINT...PRINT...PRINT...

In the printing technique invented by Gutenberg in the fifteenth century, words were formed by placing the letters one by one in guides, and when the page was complete it was coated with ink and pressed onto paper; the operation was repeated as often as necessary to produce the desired copies. As early as 1480, printing press had spread in Germany, Spain, Italy, France, England and Poland.

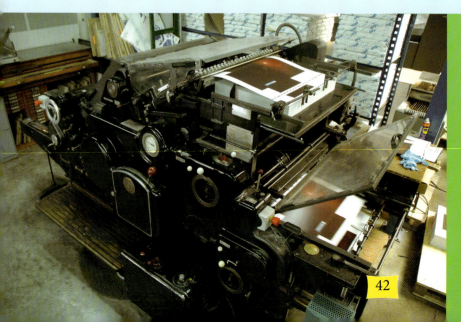

GOING DIGITAL

In modern printing systems, the entire process is guided by computer. The printer receives a compact disc that contains both the text and the digitised images. A computer interprets the information and transfers it to the machines that prepare all the printing elements based on the instructions received.

TV

The images and the sound reproduced in the television travel by waves or by cable.

THE CODE

The base of the telecommunications is the use of codes that transform sound and light, which are electromagnetic waves, in electrical signals.

MOVING IMAGES

This phenomenon, which has been known for a very long time, was applied during the nineteenth century to devices with such complex names as phenaskistiscope, praxinoscope, and fantascope, the most familiar example of which is the zootrope. This consisted of a series of illustrations placed on a cylinder that spun quickly and caused them to pass in front of a slot through which the observer watched, making the images appear to move.

TELEPHONE EXPERIMENT

MATERIAL:

- Two plastic cups or two cans. You can recycle yogurt containers or food cans.
- Thin cotton or wool string, about 6 metres long.
- Two wood sticks (you can use matchsticks)

Now look for a friend whom you want to speak with through your phone. Pull the string and ask your friend to put the cup close to his or her ear. Even if you talk softly through the cup your friend will hear you. Now ask him or her to tell you something so that you can hear. This is possible because the sound is transmitted by the string.

1. Make a hole with a screw on the base of the cup or can. Ask an adult for help.
2. Put one end of the string inside the hole of the cup, and tie one stick with two knots inside so the string doesn't come out. Do the same with the other cup.

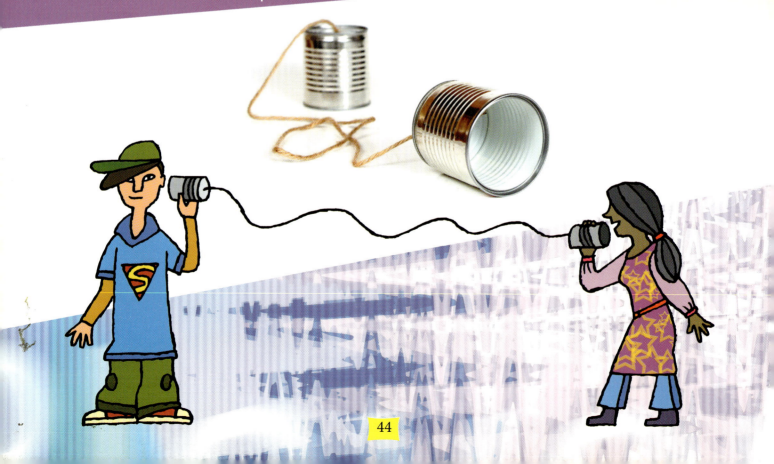

SMILE PLEASE!!

People have been fascinated by the production of images ever since prehistoric times, as demonstrated by the cave paintings found in various parts of the world; however, the artistic and small-scale methods used made them available to only a few people. Camera was such an equipment to capture moments and preserve them for life.

RECORDING AND REPRODUCING

The recording system for compact discs or CDs uses a laser to produce microscopic perforations on the disc's surface film. In the players, a low-intensity laser beam is reflected off the surface of the disc, and the changes produced in it by the perforations are "read" by light-sensitive diodes.

Did you know that...

Electronics arose as a division of electricity when Edison accidentally discovered that an electrical current flows from a hot filament. This was later identified as coming from free electrons when in the presence of another current charged with positive electricity.

FLICKERING THAT ANNOYS!!

When we see a scene of a movie or a television program on a television set, we see clearly that the image is flickering. In order to make this effect invisible, television stations broadcast twice as many images per second as necessary to produce the sensation of movement.

CAPTURING MOTION

Photography, movies, and television quickly became indispensable features of modern society. Special effects made it possible to create spectacular and unreal scenes, that were only imagined before!

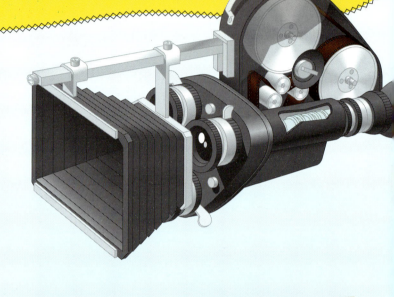

MAKE A KALEIDOSCOPE

MATERIAL:

- 2 LONG, NARROW MIRRORS
- A CARD
- CELLOTAPE
- PAPER
- OIL
- COLOURED MARBLE PAPER
- A TORCH

PROCEDURE

1. Tape the mirrors together along the long side.
2. Now tape between them a piece of card, the same size as the mirrors, so that you get a triangular shape.
3. Cover one end with a piece of paper and tape it. Smear the paper with a little oil and let it dry.
4. Now cut tiny pieces of the coloured sheets of paper and put them in the tube.
5. Make a small hole in another piece of paper. Cover the top of the tube with it and tape it as shown. Your kaleidoscope is ready.
6. Shine a torch through the oiled side of the paper, and look through the hole. Notice the colour patterns.

LET'S CREATE A RAINBOW

MATERIAL

- a glass
- water
- a large piece of paper

1. Choose a window from which sunlight is entering the room.
2. Place the glass on the window sill. Fill the glass to the brim with water. See that light falls on the water.
3. Place the white paper on the floor and receive the light refracted from the water. Can you see the rainbow colours? Which colour forms the outermost band?

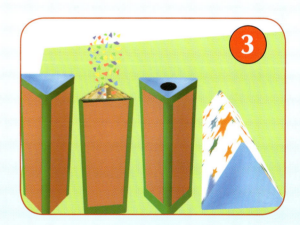

LET'S HAVE FUN WITH A COLOUR WHEEL

MATERIAL:

- cards
- a compass
- a pencil
- a paint box and a brush
- glue
- toothpicks

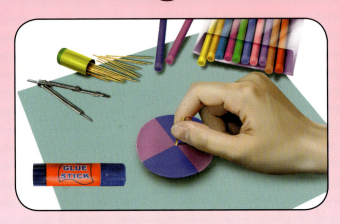

PROCEDURE

1. Draw and cut out circles of a card. Divide the circles into 4 sections and colour the sections red and green alternately.
2. Push a toothpick through the centre of the circle and fix it with glue.
3. Spin the wheel. What colour do you see?
4. Similarly make wheels with blue and red, blue and green and blue, red and green. Spin to see the effect.
5. Now make a wheel with the colours of the spectrum. You can leave out indigo. Dividing a circle into 12 sections is easier. Spin the wheel and see what happens.

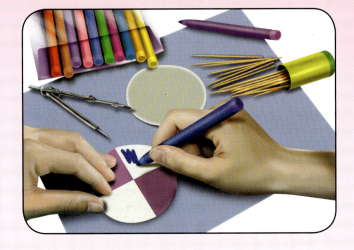

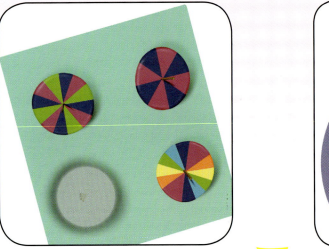

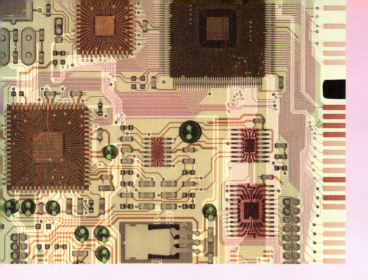

CHANGE THE CHIP
SILICON VALLEY

If your console, your watch, or your computer don't work, maybe you have to change a chip. The integrated circuits commonly called chips are small plates of silicon that contain thousands or millions of transistors.

It is a term which refers to the Southern part of Northern California, USA. It is home to many of the world's largest technology corporations, hence the name.

LOOKING FOR CHIPS

If you have any electrical device at home that is not working, ask the help of an adult to take it apart and look with a magnifying glass to see if it has a chip. Afterwards observe the transistors and the other components of the chip.

TRANSISTOR
It is the base of electronics and it is made with semiconductor materials and is used to control the electric current.

The first transistors were made of Germanium (Ge), but after we realised it was better to use Silicon (Si) because it withstands higher temperatures.

COMPUTE
AND
ORGANISE

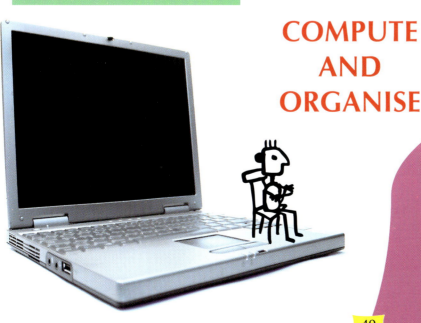

The computers are machines that receive and process data that they transform into audiovisual information. They are able to calculate and organise the information and execute instructions very quickly.

METAL BEINGS...

Although television and movies have conditioned us to think of robots as mechanical beings that appear human, any machine that can perform a task automatically without the direct intervention of a human can be considered a robot.

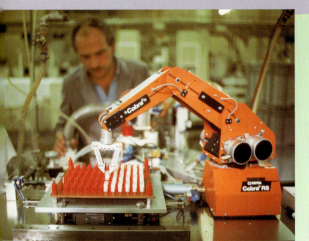

Robots can carry out tasks in surroundings that are dangerous for people (as in nuclear power plants) or that require sterile air (as in the pharmaceuticals industry).

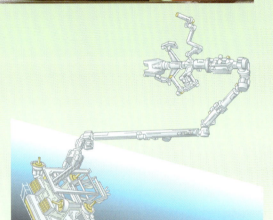

ROBOT INVASION?

Such phrases have inspired many movies and novels. But, experts say that it is only a matter of time when robots will think for themselves. It is like marrying a vacuum cleaner and then letting it nag you every day.

SPACE ROBOTS

One of the most impressive tasks that robots carry out is loading and unloading NASA's space shuttles. This involves the use of a huge articulated arm that can move items weighing several tonnes with total precision. This arm is remarkable not only for its strength, but also for the delicacy with which it manipulates precision instruments that cost many millions of dollars.

AN "ALMOST INTELLIGENT" DOG

In the last few years of the twentieth century, the Japanese company Sony developed a small robot that looked like a dog. It was named AIBO. AIBO introduction of automatic machines and robots seems to represent a loss of employment for humans; however, as time passes, the machines create more satisfying and higher-paying jobs.

DANGER!!!

Radioactive wastes are usually stored for a peroid of time until it no longer poses a hazard.

Chernobyl, Exxon Valdez, Prestige, the Gulf War...

These names represent nuclear accidents, oil spills in the sea, wars... They are environmental and social disasters related with energy from recent history.

The lady of radioactivity

Marie Curie won two Nobel prizes for her work on radioactivity. She discovered that radioactivity is a property of certain atoms that originates in their nucleus.

ALTERNATIVES TO THE ENERGY CRISIS

The possibility of running out of resources in the future and the environmental and social problems that have come from the over consumption of energy have led to energy saving measures, such as recycling and the use of renewable energies.

PHYSICS OF THE SMALL

Quantum mechanics has sparked a revolution in physics and the development of nanotechnology. The nanotubes, for example, have infinite uses from electronics to medicine.

Don't think that you'll be able to see a nanotube with a magnifying glass. They are so small that we need very powerful microscopes.

Did you know that...

30% OF ENERGY IS WASTED IN BUILDINGS OR USED INEFFICIENTLY.

The consumption of energy today is 115 times greater than during pre-history.

51

THE SPIRAL STAIR CASE OF A SNAIL

The book of life doesn't have the form of a book, instead it is like a string that revolves around itself creating a spiral. This is where all the information about life is writtern, not using ink but with chemical material.

If we pulled the DNA strings of all the cells in our body forming a straight line they would measure **17 million miles!**

There are parts of the HUMAN GENOME that no one knows the meaning of, but when we understand it to perfection, we will reconstruct the incredible trip of our evolution and cure many illnesses.

The contest OF THE CENTURY

In 2003, the contest of the human genome was over. The winners were the first group of scientists that deciphered all the genetic material of humans.

It took them 13 years!

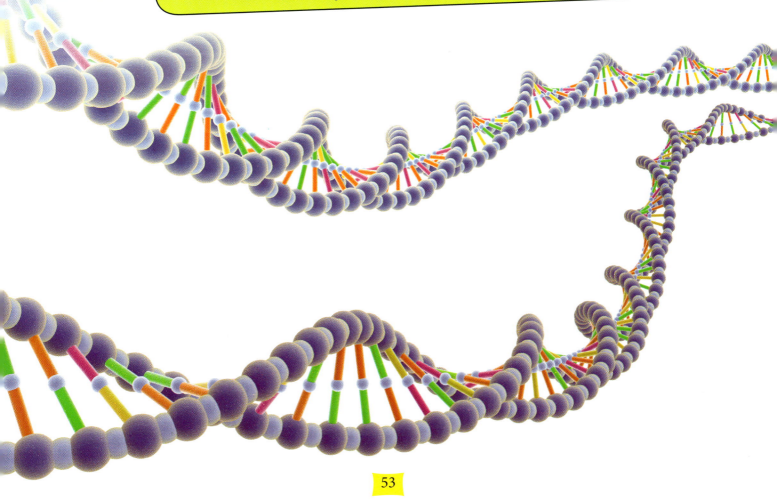

ROSALIND FRANKLIN:

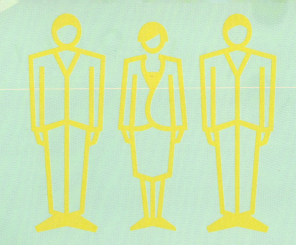

— **Dear Doctor Rosalind, is it true that without your experiments the structure of DNA would never have been discovered?**

— Frankly I don't know anyone that can take better photos of DNA than me with the technique of diffracting X-rays. And it is obvious that my pictures were the ones to reveal the mystery of their shape.

— **How did you feel when you realised that someone had stolen the results of your experiments?**

— It bothered me tremendously that my boss, Wilkins, excluded me from his research. I would have loved to share my results with the doctors Watson and Crick. But we never got along well, so I wasn't surprised at all.

— **Do you think that you deserved the Nobel prize for your work with DNA, together with your colleagues Watson, Crick, and Wilkins?**

— Yes, of course. But at that time women scientists were undervalued. Nevertheless, I am very proud for having worked on what I wanted to do and having obtained such good results.

BIOTECHNOLOGY

Today, we know the book of life of several organisms and many techniques for manipulating it. We can trim down a chapter of a fish's book and paste it onto a plant's book. This way the plant will learn to do something new, something that until now only the fish was able to do.

THE FAMOUS SHEEP DOLLY

Dolly was famous for being the first animal without a mom and dad. She was conceived in a laboratory as an exact copy of her mother.

 =

CROSS GENETIC CONTAMINATION

The information about the characters of cross genetic organisms has an incredible capacity to expand. Therefore there is a danger that using them diminishes biodiversity.

STRUGGLING AGAINST EPIDEMIC AND PLAGUES

THE STRUGGLE AGAINST SICKNESS HAS BEEN A CHALLENGE FOR ALL TIMES. KNOWING NATURE HELPS US TO LOOK FOR WAYS OF CURING THEM.

AGROECOLOGY,
BIOLOGICAL CONTROL OF THE PLAGUES

The plagues are communities of insects that take over farmers' fields and devour them entirely. To fight them we have developed some very ingenious strategies.

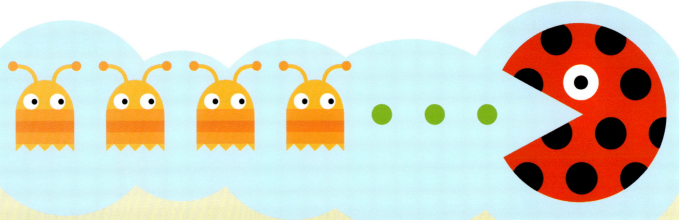

NH₂ — Cytosine (C)

O

Guanine (G)

SCENTED TRAPS

We can stop the insects from reproducing by playing with their pheromones, which are odour substances that many animals produce to attract and find a partner.

AGAINST the plagues of your house

If you have a plant at home that has been attacked by fleas, you can save it. Get as many lady bugs as you can in a box and spread them on the plant. They will eat the fleas. Use a magnifying glass to look at the fleas and lady bugs.

WITH THE INCREASING USE OF CHEMICAL INSECTICIDES WE HAVE TO WASH THE VEGETABLES VERY WELL IN ORDER TO PREVENT THEM FROM HARMING US BECAUSE THEY CAN BE TOXIC.

Chemical insecticides

Insects are able to adapt to living with insecticides and to make themselves resistant to it. That's why some insecticides stop working after a while and new ones have to be created. Also, they frequently kill lots of other species that are not plagues.

Thymine (T)

Adenine (A)

DNA: Deoxyribonucleic Acid
RNA: Ribonucleic Acid

Recombinant DNA is the result of introducing or removing parts of the original DNA chain.

YUMMY!

Cheeses, which are now made on an industrial scale, are one product of biotechnology.

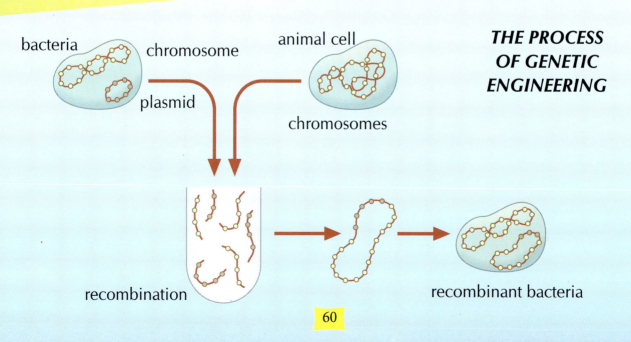

bacteria   chromosome   animal cell

plasmid

chromosomes

recombination   recombinant bacteria

THE PROCESS OF GENETIC ENGINEERING

CLONES ARE NOT EXACT COPIES!

Clones are basically the genetic identical twins. The individual clones have their own characteristics and traits.

Corn is one crop with which a fairly large number of transgenic varieties have been developed.

HUMAN CLONING!

At the end of 2001, an American laboratory succeeded in cloning human embryos for the purpose of obtaining tissues for medical purposes.

INFORMATION IN THE BRAIN

The cells that quickly transmit information in the brain are called neurons and they do it by electric impulses.

NEURON

The scientist Ramón Y Cajal identified neurons for the first time and was able to explain the functioning of the nervous system. For this discovery he won the first Nobel prize for Medicine.

Without pain

When a dentist began to use ether in order to extract his own tooth he started the use of anaesthesia that made a great advance for surgery. This medical progress has been very important for being able to make organ transplants that have saved many lives.

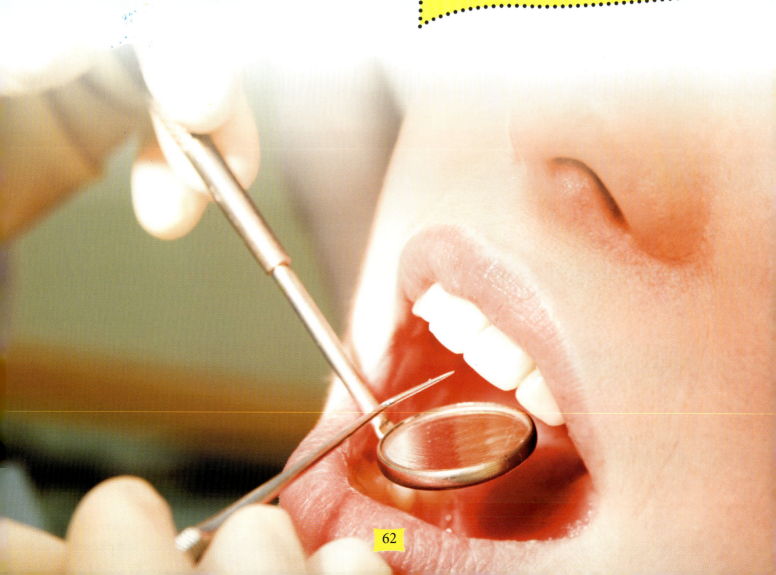

SCIENTIFIC MEDICINE

During the 19th century medicine applied scientific knowledge and methods to the art of curing, therefore giving it a scientific character. The knowledge about physics and chemistry and the advances in research on cells was fundamental for this great leap forward.

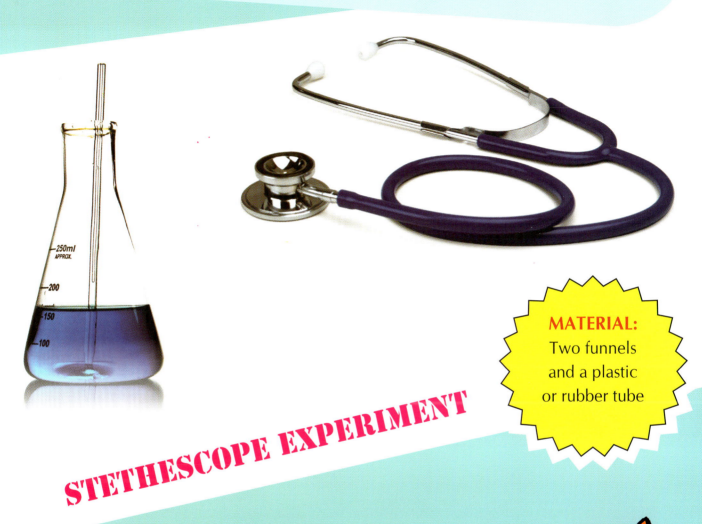

STETHESCOPE EXPERIMENT

MATERIAL:
Two funnels and a plastic or rubber tube

1. *Attach a funnel in every end of the tube.*
2. *Put one funnel onto your chest or a friend's chest.*

Do you hear the heartbeats?
And the respiration? You can also listen to the sound of your digestion if you put the funnel on your tummy. What you're doing is auscultating, like the doctors do. Almost always when we go to the doctor they auscultate us with the stethoscope. This instrument has been used in medicine since the beginning of the 19th century.

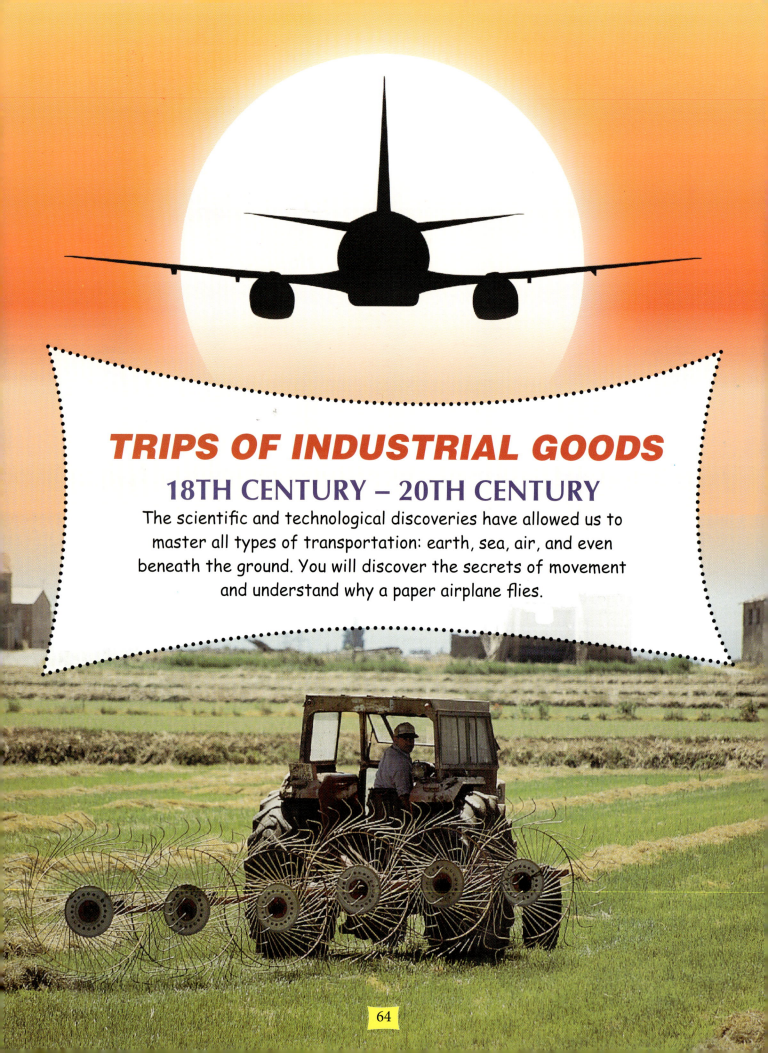

TRIPS OF INDUSTRIAL GOODS

18TH CENTURY – 20TH CENTURY

The scientific and technological discoveries have allowed us to master all types of transportation: earth, sea, air, and even beneath the ground. You will discover the secrets of movement and understand why a paper airplane flies.

Do you know why we used to draw trains with smoke?

ALL ABOARD

The train in the image is similar to the first locomotives. They had smoke coming from a chimney because the steam engine was making the trains move.

The steam engine revolutionised the way we lived and many people began to work in mechanised factories. We received food that arrived in trains and travelled in boats that did not depend on wind. Other inventions, like electricity or the airplane, have allowed us to travel beneath the ground or to fly.

From the hands to the engines

Before we invented the steam engine the transportation of goods and people was done with carts pulled by horses or with sail boats, but with this new invention it was possible to travel quicker and farther.

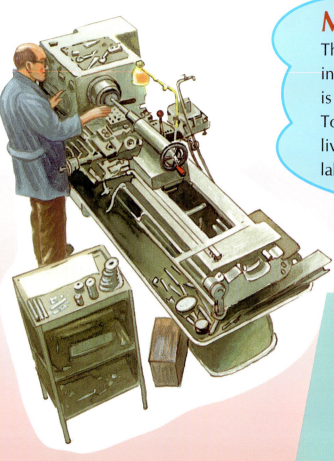

MACHINE TOOLS

The term machine is used to designate any instrument, whether simple or complex, that is capable of performing one or more actions. Tools have been used for millennia to ease the lives of human beings and have freed them from laborious duties.

HOW DO MACHINE TOOLS WORK?

In any machine tool, in addition to the motor, there are three different types of components that can be identified: a receiver, a transmission mechanism that commends the movement, and a tool or operator.

Did you know that...

Modern looms turn out fabric at high speed and with great precision.

DOMESTIC APPLIANCES

There are very affordable domestic versions of some of these tools that function with a small electric motor.

A SAWMILL

In a sawmill large logs are cut using rip saws, radial saws and longitudinal saws. Earlier, people harvested timber and used to cut them by hands. What a painstaking process?

WOOD: A MATERIAL WITH MANY VARIETIES...

The machines used in working with wood vary greatly in order to assemble or join pieces together, shaping, gluing, etc.; and finally, smoothing and polishing tools are used in the finishing process.

ON THE FARM

In developed countries it is rare to see farmers working with hand tools or with the help of animals; it is more common to see them driving a tractor, using rakes, mechanical plows, harvester or planters.

METAL AGAINST METAL!

Machinery for metalworking can be divided into three classes: machines that produce shavings or chips, that change the shape of the metal, and that physically transform metal.

Are Machines The Ultimate?

No matter how precise and automated a machine may be, there is always a person who controls how it works.

THE LATHE

The lathe is a machine with a long history; it played a crucial role in the industrialisation that took place at the end of the nineteenth century and the beginning of the twentieth. In order to understand its importance, you need only to consider that before it was invented, nuts and bolts were made by hand.

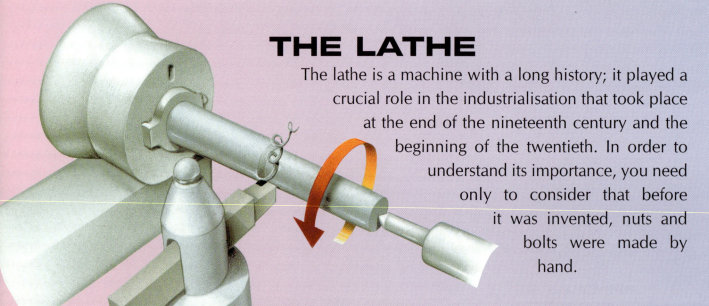

SMART MACHINES

Little by little, machines have been turning into true robots that perform their tasks automatically, and people become involved only in programming their operation, overseeing their correct functioning, and performing certain repairs.

TIME TO ASSEMBLE...

A significant amount of industrial work is done by linking operations in assembly lines comprising a series of assembly line machines that automatically work on parts that move along them.

It's true!

Robots perform their duties precisely and tirelessly; they are perfect for working in areas that present dangers to humans.

An engine that works with water

In the steam engine the heat is transformed into movement. In a boiler and the pressure of this makes the mechanism activate and move the wheels of the train, the blades of a boat, or an industrial engine.

COAL ← Remains of Plants

It was the main source of fuel until oil substituted it. We knew many sources, the extraction was cheap, and its use was simple, even for heating houses and for cooking.

Remains of living things → OIL

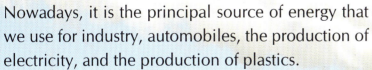

Nowadays, it is the principal source of energy that we use for industry, automobiles, the production of electricity, and the production of plastics.

The combustion of oil and of coal causes the emission of CO_2, a gas that increases the greenhouse gas effect and the global warming of the planet.

Oil has been the cause of economic crisis and wars.

A VALUABLE RAW MATERIAL

Since petroleum derivatives are used so extensively, as fuel it is easy to overlook their use as raw materials in producing important products as plastics and synthetic rubber. And that is not the end of the uses for petroleum; it is also used in many other processes in the organic chemical industry, as in the production of synthetic fibres and the pharmaceuticals industry.

NATURAL GAS

Natural gas is a fossil fuel that was formed much like petroleum. In the natural state it is a mixture of gases, primarily methane, but it also includes undesirable products that must be removed before distributing it.

HYDROCARBONS

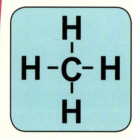

Natural gas are sources of raw materials including methane, which is used in manufacturing varied and important products as nitrogen fertilisers, lamp black, ammonia, and anaesthetics.

FINITE OR INFINITE?

Even though new deposits have been discovered in recent years and old ones are being exploited more efficiently, fossil fuels are a finite resource.

Oil consumption is highest in USA. The biggest oil producer is Saudi Arabia, followed by Russia.

COMBUSTION

Before doing this experiment, ask for the help of an adult.

METAL:

- A deep dish
- A pitcher of water
- A candle
- A box of matches
- A narrow glass that is bigger than the candle

1. Place the dish on the table and fill it with water to the top without spilling.

2. Put the candle in the dish, inside the water, so that it stands up.

3. Light the candle and observe how the combustion process takes place: light and heat are given off.

4. Cover the candle with the glass and observe what happens.

You will see the flame goes out little by little and the water level rises in the glass.

Why does this occur?

Combustion is a chemical reaction that needs a combustible substance that in this case is the wax of a candle, and the presence of oxygen. Covering the candle with the cup consumes all the oxygen, for this reason the candle goes out and the water level rises to take the space once occupied by the oxygen.

AN ENORMOUS GREENHOUSE

Greenhouses are a type of house constructed with glass where plants grow. The glass lets the heat of the sun pass, maintaining a constant temperature and retaining the humidity. The Earth is a gigantic greenhouse where the gases of the atmosphere would be comparable to the glass of a greenhouse.

ALERT ! !

Greenhouse gases contribute to GLOBAL WARMING! The average temperature of the Earth has increased by 0.8°C since the last 100 years. Climates are changing, glaciers are melting, diseases are spreading and biodiversity is being lost.

Bicycles

Did you know that...

- The smallest bicycle ever created had wheels made from silver coins.
- Half of all parts of a typical bicycle are in the chain!
- There are roughly 1 billion bicycles in the world today.

TO SUIT ALL TASTES

At first there were different types of bicycles, some faster, others more comfortable, but none was better than another, they simply had different people using them such as mailmen, women or sportsmen.

Legs that
LIGHT UP

When you pedal during the night you can illuminate your path with a dynamo, a small gadget that goes on the wheel of the bicycle. This is formed by magnets and threads and, thanks to a phenomenon called "electromagnetic induction", it transforms the mechanical energy of your legs into electric energy and makes it function as a headlight.

Who FLEW first?

In the race for obtaining the title of the first flight we have the Wright brothers in the United States and the French-Brazilian, Santos Dumont. Although the Wright brothers managed to fly first, they needed a machine to launch the airplane, whereas Santos Dumont managed to fly without the help of any other machine.

Crossing Atlantic...

The first to fly over the Atlantic was Charles Lindbergh and first woman to fly was Amelia Earhart.

Imaginary interview with...
Leonardo da Vinci
(1452-1519)

Architect
Sculptor
Scientist
Musician
Engineer
Mathematician
Inventor
Designer
Botanist

GENIUS

— *Dear Leonardo, it is an honour to interview - the "master of the arts". To begin I would like to know what do you do exactly.*

— Thank you very much for calling me this, I never imagined that my works were worth so much. I love many aspects of science, technology, sculpture, architecture, and music. Ah... and also drawing and painting. You know the painting of Mona Lisa? Well I painted it...it took me four years more or less to make it, but I still think it's pretty.

— *My goodness! Leonardo, you do many things. It is said that besides being very wise, you are also a great inventor. Have you invented some means of transportation?*

— Observing and studying the birds I wondered if human beings could fly too. I tried to create some types of flying machines, but my dream of flying was not realised. To move more quickly, this time on the ground, I thought about a machine with two wheels that I could sit on...I believe today you call it a bicycle.

— *What is your true passion? Art or science?*

— My goodness, I never separate the two things. Science has art and art has science. It's a pity that scientists today are not more artistic.

FOUR-CYCIE
ENGINES

One internal combustion engine built by the German technician Nikolaus Otto in 1876 became the model on which the future gasoline motors would be based.

During the infancy of the automobile, many types of motors were tried in vehicles with three and four wheels.

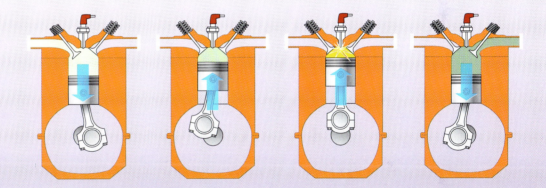

THE FIRST MOTORS

The first fuel used for an internal combustion engine was gunpowder, but that was quickly abandoned in favour of other fuels such as vapour of turpentine and hydrogen.

DIESEL

Diesel motors revolutionised heavy transport of humans and goods starting in the twentieth century, and they facilitated the introduction of new and powerful locomotives.

NEW AGE MOTORS

Designers of new motors will have to be more conscious of energy efficiency and pollution reduction.

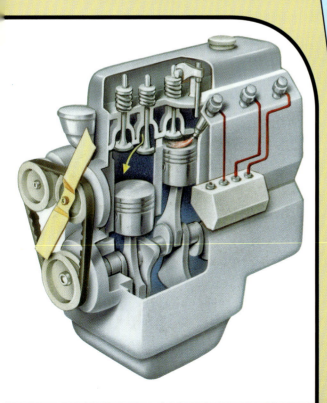

ADVANTAGES OF DIESEL

Because of the way it burns the fuel, the diesel motor is more economical and less polluting than other internal combustion engines. Improvements in the injection system and in construction materials have made diesel motors almost as light as gasoline engines, and they can now compete with them in power and acceleration.

TRAFFIC SIGNAL

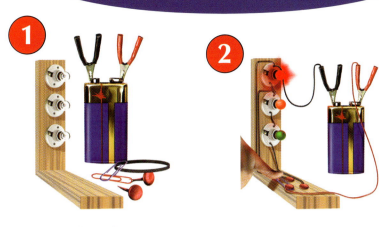

Material

- 3 torch bulbs and sockets
- a 9-volt battery
- 2 battery clips
- an L-shaped wooden board
- 4 board pins
- a paper clip
- same insulated wire
- red, green and orange colour paints

PROCEDURE

1. Make a 3-way switch with the 4 board pins and the paper clip, as shown, at the base of the wooden board.
2. Fix the torch bulbs as shown. Paint them red, orange and green so that they look like traffic lights.
3. Wire them to the battery through the 3-way switch. The bulbs are connected in parallel. So they can be switched on separately.
4. Connect the switch alternately to the three board pins to operate the traffic signal.

SAVE THE MONEY!

Once people solved the problem of the type of current to produce, one of the cheapest ways to produce it was to take advantage of running water to power the generators in order to take better advantage of the power of the differences in water level. Hydraulic turbines were designed for the conditions of each reservoir.

Canada is the largest producer of hydropower in the world and USA is the second. It's an energy that is clean, eco-friendly and renewable.

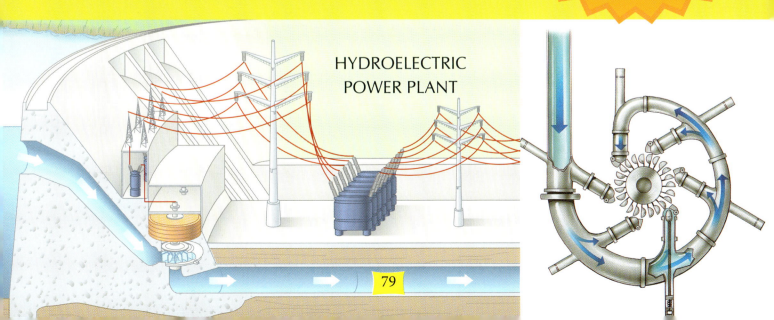

HYDROELECTRIC POWER PLANT

TO MAKE A WATER WHEEL

Material

- An empty plastic bottle
- Two corks
- Small pieces of plastic or wood
- A knitting needle
- A pair of scissors
- Thread
- An empty matchbox

1. Cut four plastic or wooden fins.
2. Make four slits in the sides of the cork, and one hole through the middle of the cork.
3. Push the fins into the slits in the cork.
4. Make a hole at the bottom of the plastic bottle.
5. Push the knitting needle through the cork with the fins into the bottle and out through the hole at the bottom.
6. Now push the point of the knitting needle into the other cork. The needle should be able to turn round inside the cork.
7. Hold the bottle and put your water wheel under a tap and watch it turn round.
8. Tie a long thread with a matchbox on the other end to the second cork. As the water wheel turns, it will lift up the matchbox.

1

2

3

THE MIGHTY WIND

Wind-generated electricity is produced very cleanly and without consuming non-renewable resources; however, in some cases people criticise the location of the wind farms in areas of ecological or scenic interest.

Germany produces 8750 MV of electrical energy from wind. Wind energy is basically a transformed form of Sun's energy.

THE BLAZING SUN...

The Sun gives off five million tonnes of its mass as radiation, and even though just one ten-millionth of that energy reaches the Earth, today it is a promising source of energy - the solar energy.

In one hour more sunlight falls on the Earth than what is used by the entire population in one year.

READY FOR TAKE OFF

In order for a plane that weighs so much to fly, it needs tremendous force through the air. The secret is the form of the wings and the velocity. After the push that the turbines give to the plane the wind passes through the wings and, thanks to their formation, the air pushes the plane upwards.

1. Put a mark in the middle of the longest part of the paper, folding and unfolding it. Now fold the two tips of the top part as indicated in the drawing.
2. Fold the sheet down, but not in the middle, so that the tip does not arrive to the base of the sheet.
3. Fold the top corners until the marked line from part 1, as indicated in the figure.
4. Fold the triangle upwards that appears below the fold of the marking from step 3.
5. Fold in the middle, on the line marked in part 1.
6. Now fold the wings as shown in the drawing.
7. Launch your paper airplane and observe it!

Did you know that...

Commercial airlines prohibit to carry mercury thermometers because mercury reacts with aluminium, and can badly damage the plane.

 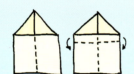

As our paper airplane is light, it does not need a wing like a real plane nor a turbine to accelerate it. Your force is like the turbine of a real plane.

THE DIRIGIBLE, THE FIRST SERIOUS ATTEMPT!

Currently there are several projects underway to reintroduce the dirigible as which is an aluminium cigar shaped zeppelin that was a success in 1900, as a way of carrying cargo, especially over moderate distances, because they don't need much room to land.

DOGGED BY TRAGEDY

The dirigible balloon or the zeppelin, as it was also known in honour of its inventor, showed for almost 30 years that it could be used not only for short and moderate flights, but also for ocean crossings, with the added advantage that it did not need specially prepared areas for takeoff and landing. It was successful as a means of transporting people and goods until a series of accidents capped by a major tragedy caused them to be outlawed. The cause was that the balloon was filled with hydrogen, a gas that is much lighter than air but extremely flammable. Presentday dirigibles, used especially for advertising purposes, use helium, which is much more expensive but harmless.

Charles Lindbergh's Plane!

To make a Whirl-fan

PROCEDURE

1. Cut teeth in the circumference of the tin disk.
2. Bend the teeth a little for better effects (see picture).
3. Bend the knitting needle with the pliers and push in the cork to make a handle.
4. Pivot the toothed wheel on the free end of the needle.
5. Now hold it above a candle flame and see how the wheel revolves.

MATERIAL:

- A thin circular tin disk like those used in tinned food packs
- A pair of scissors or cutters
- A knitting needle
- A pliers
- A cork
- A candle
- A matchbox

FIRE FOR FLYING

The warmer the air the lighter it is. That's why the hot-air balloons manage to go up, because the heat of the fire warms up the air in the balloon and it becomes less heavy.

THE HOT-AIR BALLOONS AS WELL AS BLIMPS, MANAGE TO KEEP IN THE AIR DUE TO THE ARCHIMEDES PRINCIPLE.

ELECTRIC TRANSPORTATION

The first trolleys worked with steam engines, but later a system of high cables allowed them to function with electricity.

AN ELEVATOR FOR BOATS

How can you make a low level river navigable? You can utilise a type of elevator called a lock. The boat enters, the floodgate closes to fill the lock with water, and when it is at the same level as the other side of the lock, the second floodgate opens and the boat can continue sailing.

MODERN TRANSPORTATION

Electric trains are the most ecologically sound and economical modern means of transportation.

RAIL ROADS

Railway tracks expand in summer and contract in winter. Therefore, small gaps are left in between tracks to allow movement.

The invention of the railroad modified the countryside and the customs of millions of people throughout the world.

MODEL OF A RAILWAY SIGNAL

PROCEDURE

1. Draw this frog shape on the cardboard.
2. Cut it out. Make a slot in the belly.
3. Loop the rubber band around the frog's belly.
4. Twist the loop twice with the hairpin, or till tight.
5. Cut out a very small piece of sellotape. Stick one part underneath the frog's hind legs. Stick the hairpin to the other part of the tape.
6. The band will try to untwist and pull the hairpin. This will make the frog jump.

MATERIAL
- An empty barrel of a ball point pen
- A nail
- Insulated wire
- A 9-volt battery
- Sellotape
- An on-off switch
- A cardboard box
- A 6-inch wooden scale
- Coloured paper
- Thread

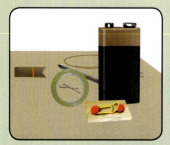

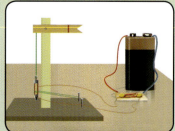

WITHOUT FORCE NOTHING CHANGES

NEWTON'S FIRST LAW:

When you shoot an arrow with an arc, why does it continue moving forward? Isaac Newton answered: "Any object that is moving in a straight line remains like this forever, unless 'something' stops it. And every object that is stopped will continue to be without movement unless 'something' makes it move."

NEWTON'S SECOND LAW:

"The force required to move or to stop anything depends on its mass and on how fast you want it to move." To understand better the relationship between force and mass you can push a cart full of suitcases and afterwards push it empty. Have you noticed any difference? To move or to stop the full cart that has more mass, more force is necessary than with the one that is empty and that has less mass.

NEWTON'S THIRD LAW:

"The mutual forces of action and reaction between two bodies are equal, opposite and collinear."

Feeling the force

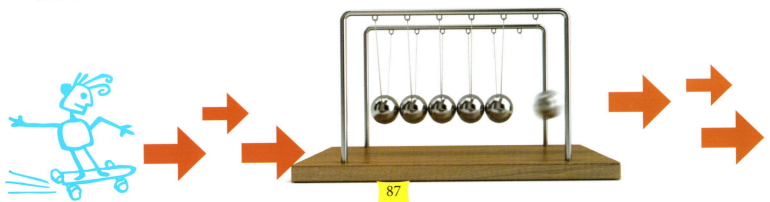

A stubborn coin

MATERIAL
- A glass
- A postcard
- A coin

PROCEDURE

1. Place the postcard on top of the glass.
2. Put the coin in the centre of the card.
3. Now flick the card away with a quick hit. What happens to the coin? The stubborn coin refuses to leave its position of rest and drops into the glass.

Try a similar experiment: Pull a tablecloth off a table very quickly leaving all the dishes in place. MAGIC!!

The greater the inertia of an object, the harder it is to move!

1

2

3

Bouncing and bouncing back

Always when you apply a force to something, this thing applies a force back onto you.

But this does not mean that if you hit the ground it will hit you back. If for example you are playing soccer and the following happens:

- **HIT THE BALL**
  The ball will go in the direction of the wall or goal.

- **THE BALL BOUNCES ON THE WALL**
  The wall "hits" the ball, and that is why it bounces back to you.

FORCE = MASS X ACCELERATION

FORCE OF GRAVITY!
It depends on the masses of the objects and the distance between the centres of the objects.

Did you know that...

On Earth objects don't really remain in motion, because friction slows them down and gravity pulls them toward the ground.

WHY DOES THE MARBLE STOP?

According to Newton's first law, if you push a marble it should move in a straight line until someone or something stops it. But there is a force that always acts when something is rubbed called the force of friction.

If we look with a magnifying glass, we can see that there are very big irregularities like the sand on the ground.

Imaginary interview with...
Isaac NEWTON
(164 3 - 172 7)

— *Hello, Sir Isaac Newton, I feel much honoured to interview the "father of classical mechanics". Why do they call you this?*

—Because with my laws of motion I have contributed enormously to this area of physics..

— *Sir Newton, do you like apples?*

— What a strange question! But I know why you ask me this. It is because of the story they tell about how I started to study universal gravity, that force that attracts us to the ground and that does not let us fly away. They say that I was under an apple tree and that when an apple fell on my head I wondered why things fall.

— *Is it true?*

—Well...the truth is that I was taking a nap and I don't remember very well. But what is important in the story is that I was a great observer of nature and that, because of these observations, I asked myself various questions that I was able to answer. Excuse me but I have to go. It's almost time for tea and some friends baked me an apple pie that I don't want to get cool.

—*Enjoy your tea and thank you very much.*

ACTION AND REACTION UNDER YOUR FEET

Take some steps paying attention to your feet. To walk, you step down and push the ground backwards. Then the ground pushes you forward. Thanks to action and reaction that we manage to walk!

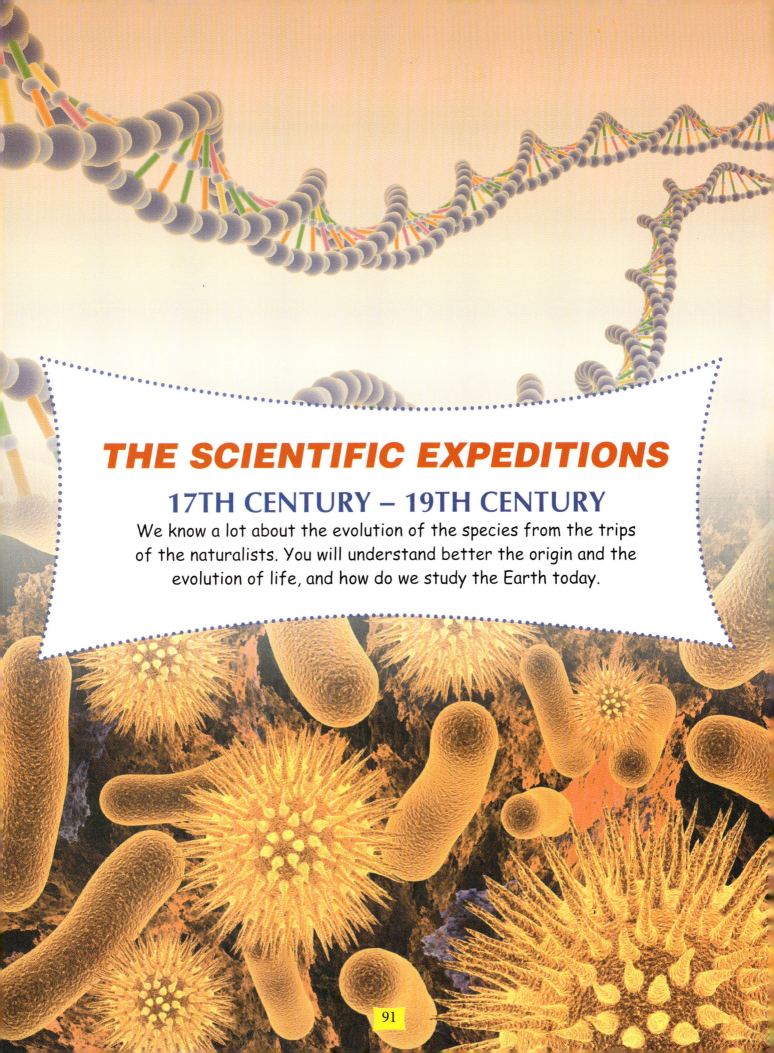

THE SCIENTIFIC EXPEDITIONS

17TH CENTURY – 19TH CENTURY

We know a lot about the evolution of the species from the trips of the naturalists. You will understand better the origin and the evolution of life, and how do we study the Earth today.

THE SCIENTIFIC EXPEDITIONS

WITHOUT DOUBT, THERE IS NO PROGRESS (DARWIN)

Snails, beetles, shells, butterflies, leaves, fossils... The naturalists passed the day collecting elements of nature. They travelled through the entire world to add to their collections and to know the species of the whole planet.

The interest in describing nature was especially in fashion among the European upper classes of the 17th and 19th century.

You need order

To be able to study so many collections the naturalists needed to organise them, to give names to species and to look for a way to classify them. This is how taxonomy emerged, the science that classifies species.

Did you know that...

Using a magnifying glass, look for four differences and two similarities between the beetles 1, 2, and 3

1

2

3

Naturalists, fish, and deserts

On the coast of Peru passes a cold ocean current rich in plankton that has created deserts and important schools of fish. It's called the Humboldt Current in honour of the naturalist who discovered it.

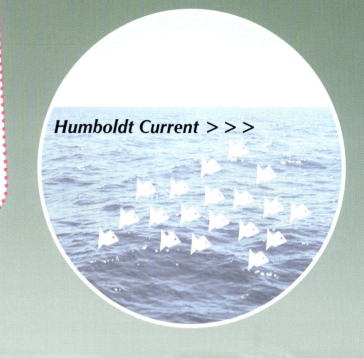

Humboldt Current > > >

The Beagle

was a boat whose objective was to travel the world to improve maps. The trip lasted five years, and they discovered incredible places!

An intrude into the expedition of the Beagle

Charles Darwin convinced the expedition of the Beagle to let him join the expedition, and he didn't lose any time and took advantage of it. He returned with boxes full of reptiles, fish and colourful birds.

As there was not even a free bed in the Beagle, Charles had to sleep during the trip in a hammock hanging in the stern!

REVEALING THE SECRET OF THE EVOLUTION OF THE SPECIES.

When putting his collections in order, Darwin discovered that they contained a secret that would revolutionise the world:

The species have kept changing with time and those that we know now are products of evolution.

Butterflies adapting to factories

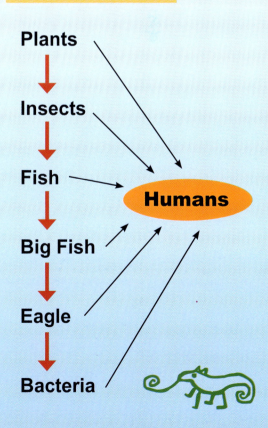

SURVIVAL OF THE FITTEST!

In the birch forests of England lived many white butterflies that, when camouflaged among the trees, prevented the birds from eating them. When the trunks went dark because of the smoke of the factories, the butterflies that were born black survived and, with time, the white ones disappeared.

CHARLES DARWIN:

The characteristics that help us survive stay and the ones that are harmful or do not provide any advantage for survival are eliminated. This means that there is a "natural selection" of the individuals that are better adapted to their environment.

Food Chains

Plants

Insects

Fish

Big Fish

Eagle

Bacteria

Humans

THE HISTORY OF LIFE ON OUR PLANET

From the time of the emergence of life on our planet, some 3.5 to 3.6 billion years — or perhaps even more — have passed. Evolution has been going on since that moment, and it has resulted in increasingly complex organisms.

THE ARCHEAN AGE

This is the oldest epoch, since it began some 3.6 billion years ago. It seems that there was great volcanic activity, huge storms, and very severe erosion of exposed land. This is the time when the first organisms appeared.

THE PROTEROZOIC AGE

This age began around 1.6 billion years ago. The formation of the most ancient glaciers took place during this time. The sea became populated with worms, jellyfish, and sponges, along with various types of aquatic plants.

THE PALEOZOIC ERA

This era began some 600 million years ago. At the beginning it was warm; afterward, however, the dryness increased, and new glaciers were formed. followed by reptiles, and, toward the end, the first dinosaurs appeared.

THE MESOZOIC ERA

This era began around 230 million years ago. This is the era in which the first birds and mammals appeared, and it was the highest point in the existence of the dinosaurs, which became extinct at the end of the Mesozoic era.

THE CENOZOIC ERA

The Cenozoic era began around 65 million years ago, and it included several periods of glaciation. The continents were taking on their present shape.

SAVED BY THEIR FACE?

Samurai crabs are called Heikegani in Japan...

The number of samurai crabs has increased because nobody eats them. There is a legend that says the Japanese warriors who died in a battle became crabs.

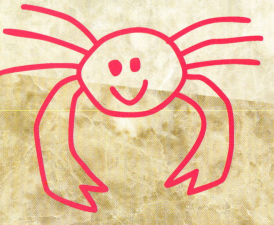

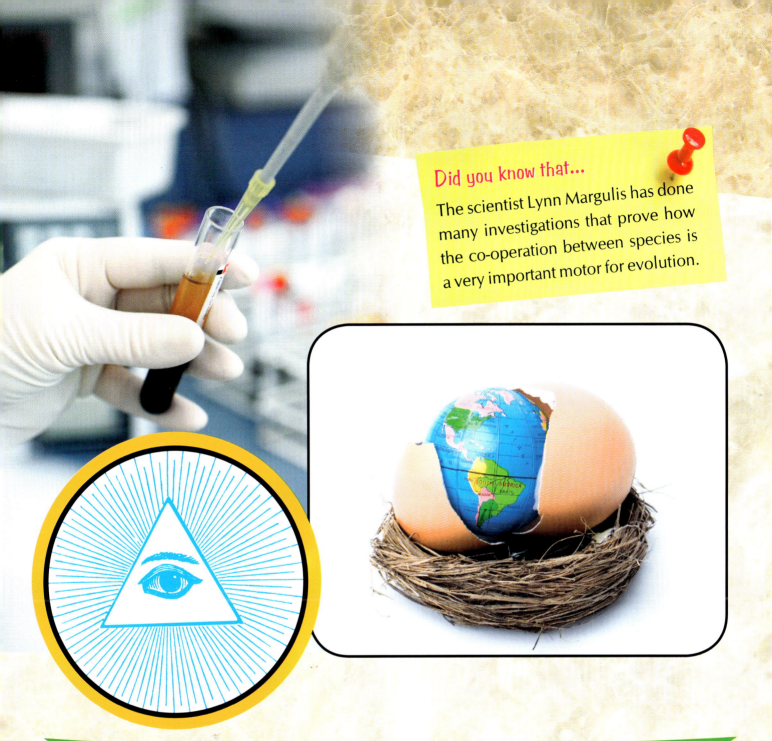

Why the theory of natur al selection was a revolution?

It contradicted the beliefs of that period. Then it was said that the Earth had suffered great changes caused by catastrophes, in which God destroyed the world to create another new one, every time more perfect.

CO-OPERATION, THE MOTOR OF EVOLUTION

Natural selection is not the only process of evolution: the union between two or more species has also given rise to new species.

Guide and digger

In the association between a fish and a blind prawn, the prawn excavates a lair where they will both be able to live. In exchange, the fish guides the prawn in the search of food.

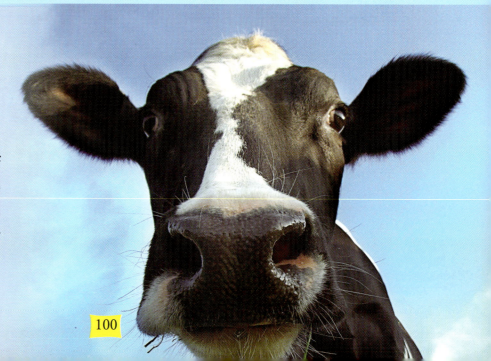

THE COWS

The cows and the rest of ruminants can digest the grass thanks to thousands of bacteria that live in their digestive system.

Gigantic worms:

Are they imaginary or real? The gigantic tube worms measure about 10 feet long and do not have eyes, mouth, or anus. They manage to survive in the dark depths of the ocean thanks to their union with bacteria.

THE TOOTHPICK BIRD!

The tiny blackbird plover eats the morsels INSIDE the African crocodile's mouth! A special bond or what?

TWO - WAY SYSTEM!

The clownfish feeds on those that can be harmful to sea anemone, and fecal matter fertilises the anemone. The stinging tentacles of sea anemones protect clownfishes and their eggs from predators.

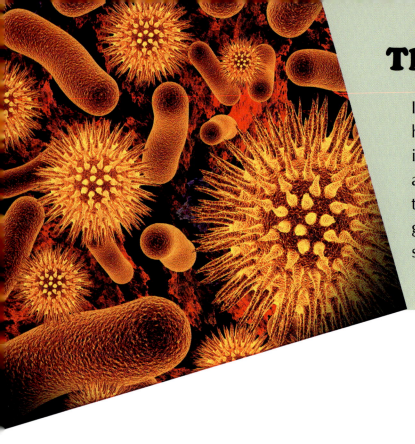

The first form of life

If life can only come from living matter, how did the first living creature appear? It is believed that about 4,000 million years ago, when there was not even a fly on Earth, there was only inert matter that evolved and gave rise to the first living creature that was similar to a bacterium.

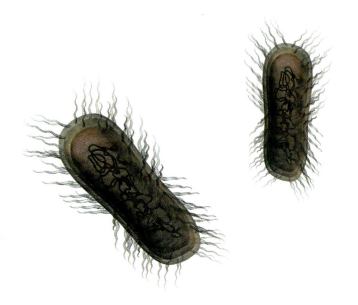

At the bottom of the sea

We believe that life could have started at the bottom of the oceans, where there are chimneys of the hot volcanic waters that come out.

BACTERIA TRAVELLERS

The theory that the origins of life are extraterrestrial has reemerged with the discovery of a Martian meteor that had bacteria in its interior.

EXPERIMENT

Things are not always what they seem. But ... where does life come from

Material:

- Two empty bottles
- A piece of gauze
- Two bits of fresh meat

1. Put a piece of meat in each of the bottles.
2. Cover one of the bottles with the gauze. It is important that it remains very well closed.
3. Leave them some days in a place where you can find flies (near a window, the balcony, the yard...).
4. Observe the bottles after 3-4 days.

3-4 days Later

You will see that in the meat of the open bottle worms have appeared spontaneously. Where did the worms come from? From the eggs that the flies leave on the meat, after waiting a little, you will see how the larvae will turn into flies. In the closed bottle larvae do not appear, because the flies have not been able to leave their eggs.

THE QUEENS OF EARTH

The bacteria were the first inhabitants of the Earth and they lived here alone for more than 2,000 million years.

The bacteria evolved to form beings that were much more complex, such as plants, fungi, animals, etc.

EMBRYOS OF DIFFERENT ANIMALS

shark	salamander	lizard	chicken	pig	rabbit	human

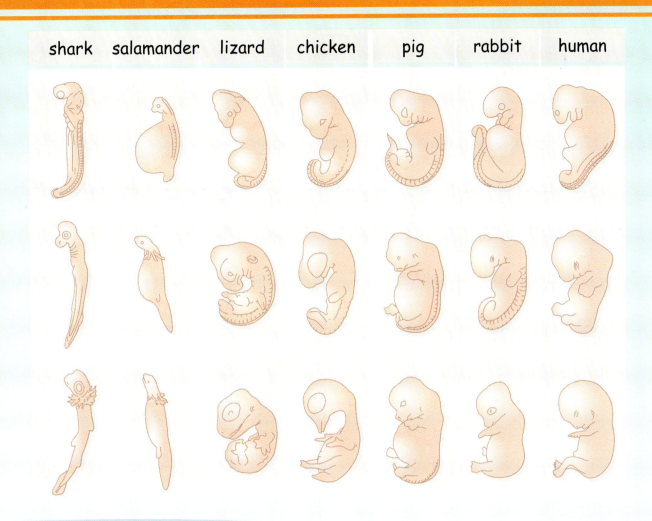

With multicelled animals that reproduce sexually, the starting point is the zygote, which results from the union of a spermatozoid and an ovule. From that moment on, the organism begins to develop, first by duplicating that initial cell and then dividing, in succession, the resulting cells until a multicelled mass of undefined shape is created. As growth continues, it resembles more and more the final adult form.

from zygote to adult

Did you know that...

Growth rings in a tree appear in the trunk every year. Dendrochrondogy or tree-ring dating is the scientific method to determine the age of a tree

Stems that climb

Whenever you see a bean plant or a honeysuckle, imagine how the stem attaches to the pole or other support. These creeping stems are called twiners or climbers. Other stalks climb by means of clinging roots, such as climbing ivy, of tendrils,
such as vines, or of thorns, as with blackberry bushes.

Did you know that...
Potatoes are swollen underground sections of stalk and the stem of an onion is in the shape of a bulb.

WHY DO WE LOOK LIKE OUR PARENTS?

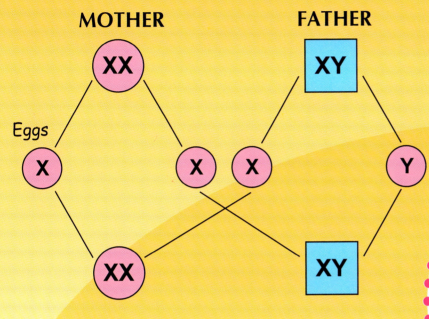

MOTHER

FATHER

Eggs

Sperms

Among parents, children, brothers, and sisters we always find resemblance and differences. The similar traits are those that we have inherited from our parents, and the different ones, are those that generate diversity.

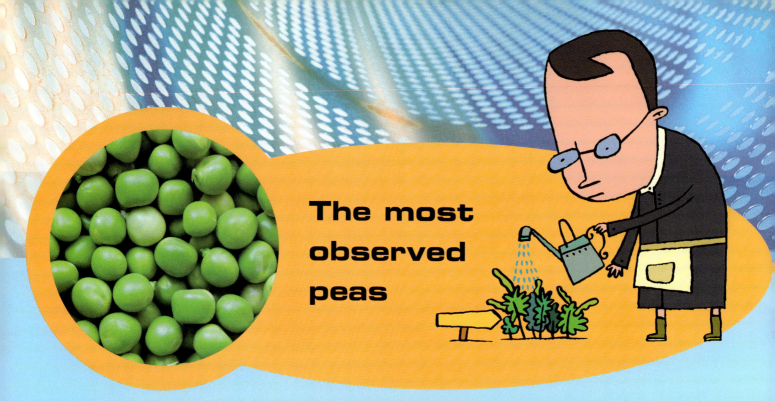

The most observed peas

Mendel was a friar who passed all his free time growing and observing peas. He wanted to discover how the traits of parents to children were transmitted. He figured it out and described the rules of inheritance.

Mice with dominant characters

A female brown mouse is bred with a white male mouse. If brown colour is the dominant trait, all the children would then be brown even if they had the information of the father's white hair.

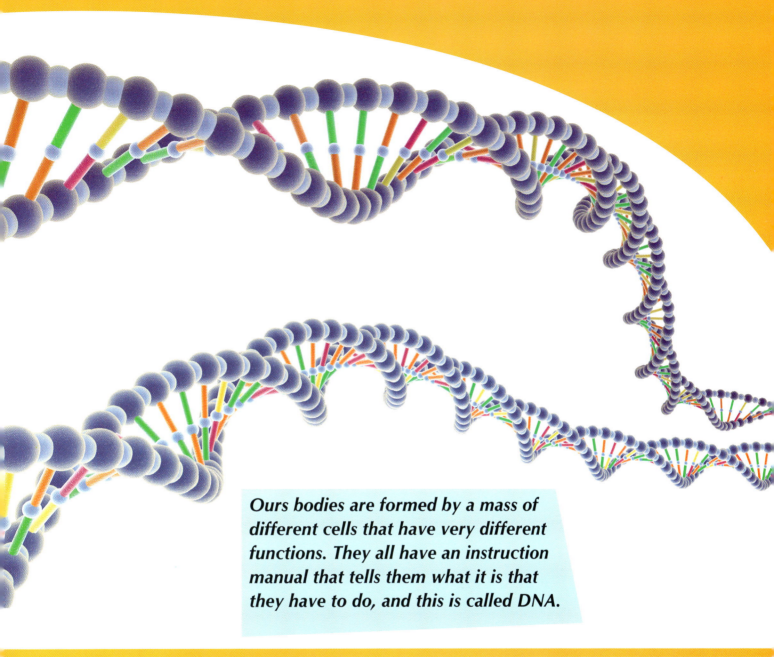

Ours bodies are formed by a mass of different cells that have very different functions. They all have an instruction manual that tells them what it is that they have to do, and this is called DNA.

WHAT'S THAT?

In the nucleus of each cell, the DNA molecule is packaged into thread-like structures called chromosomes. They come in pairs; our body has 23 pairs = 46 chromosomes.

109

EXPERIMENT:
Do the seeds know how to orient themselves in space?

MATERIAL

- Two big jars of glass, one with a cover
- Two pitchers of water
- A bowl with water
- Paper napkins
- Dry beans

1. Let some beans soak all night.
2. Roll several paper napkins up and put them in each of the jars.
3. Name the jars: jar A and jar B.
4. Put a bean in every jar, between the paper and the wall, without going to the bottom.
5. Put some water to moisten the napkins. Leave it in a warm place.
6. After two days a small root comes out.
7. After two more days, the root continues down and the plant starts to sprout.
8. When the roots are about one inch long, cover up the jar B, close it well and turn it around.
9. Three or four days afterwards observe your plants well. .

You will observe that the plant of the jar A will have turned into a sprout with leaves. In jar B the plant will have turned around alone, and you will see that the roots and sprouts have changed directions. You can see how the seeds are oriented in space thanks to the effect of gravity.

CHARACTERISTICS

The genotype is the genetic make-up of an individual based on one or more characteristics, for example, the genes that determine eye color.

Mendel founded the science of genetics by discovering the laws of heredity.

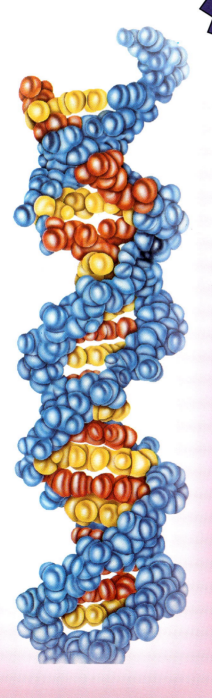

The word heredity comes from the Latin word haerentia, which means things that are linked together or belonging; the word genetics comes from the Greek genesis, which means origin or creation.

Did you know that...

In order for protein synthesis to take place, the DNA produces a messenger whose job it is to deliver the orders. The messenger is the RNA-m (messenger RNA); it is an elongated macromolecule that carries copies of the information from the DNA.

THE SUPERIOR

Gregor Mendel (1822–1884) was the grandson of a gardener, and his parents worked on a small farm; hence his interest in plants. After his studies, he entered an Augustine monastery in 1834, where he spent decades studying hybridization, especially with his famous peas. When he was appointed superior in 1864, he had to give up his experiments, which fell into oblivion until "rediscovered" by the Englishman Correns.

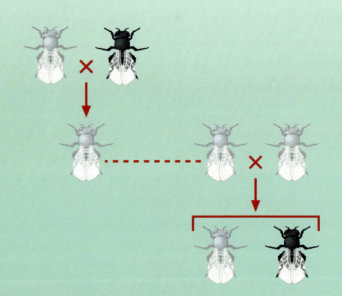

MENDEL'S FIRST LAW

When two pure strains that differ in only one characteristic are combined, all their descendants are the same.

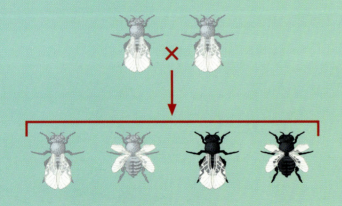

MENDEL'S SECOND LAW

When two hybrid individuals are crossed (generation 2, which is the product of generation 1) the descendants exhibit the phenotypes of the first generation in a fixed proportion.

MENDEL'S THIRD LAW

It deals with the matter of dominance, where one has dominant genes and the other has recessive genes.

Imaginary interview with...
Charles Lyell:
(164 3 - 172 7)

—**Mr. Lyell, since you study the history of Earth, do you think that Earth has changed with time?**

-Absolutely, I think that the Earth has kept on transforming with the years but very slowly.

—**Then, are you against the science of catastrophism?**

—Clearly, I can't make head or tail of those ideas! They say that the great changes in Earth have been caused by great catastrophes, in which God destroyed the world to create it again, every time more perfect.

— **Do you know that Charles Darwin adores you and says that your book 'Principles of Geology' has made him change his way of looking at the world?**

—I suppose that what he liked bout my book is the idea about actualism, which says that the natural processes that acted in the past are the same ones that act now, so if we understand the current natural phenomena, we will be able to reconstruct the history of Earth.

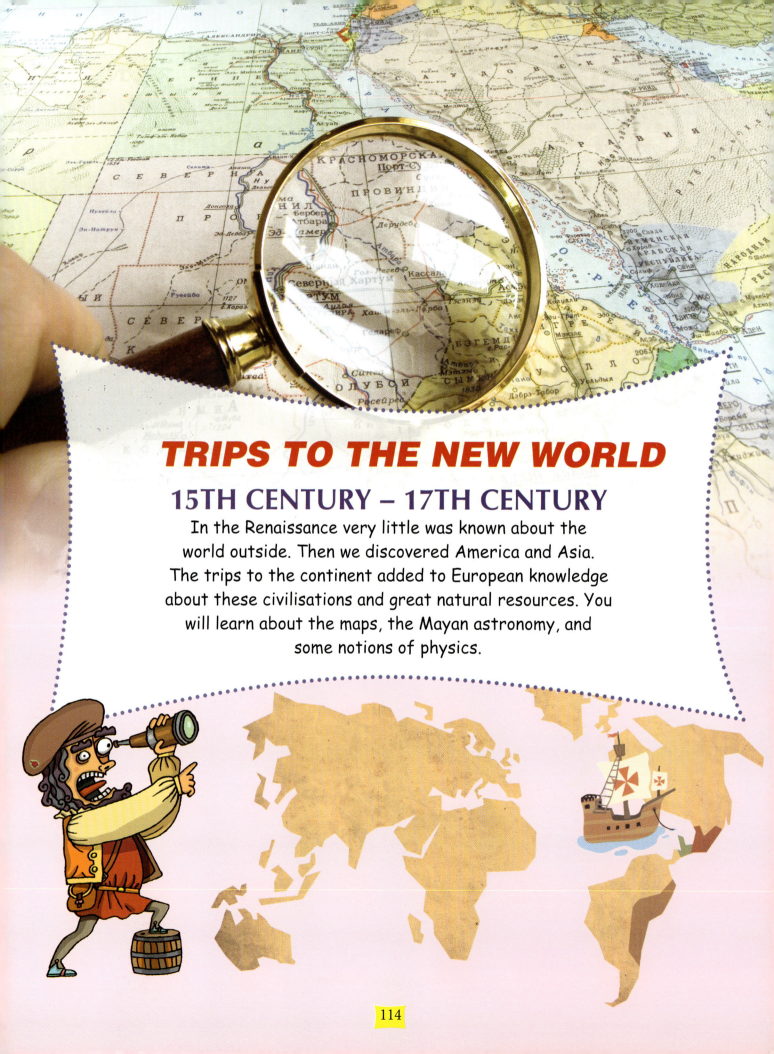

TRIPS TO THE NEW WORLD

15TH CENTURY – 17TH CENTURY

In the Renaissance very little was known about the world outside. Then we discovered America and Asia. The trips to the continent added to European knowledge about these civilisations and great natural resources. You will learn about the maps, the Mayan astronomy, and some notions of physics.

The sailor Rodrigo de Triana is known in history for the famous phrase that he said when he saw mainland from the Pinta ship.

LAND, AHOY!!!

STARTING ANEW!

With the trips to America we learned about new plants for medicine and for food. We also processed gold, silver and minerals of the new continent, but with the conquests most of the books that recorded the story and the knowledge of the pre-Hispanic civilisations were lost.

Christopher Columbus' father was a weaver and he wanted his son to become one too. But Columbus wanted to sail. So, he became a sailor at the age of 10.

A STONE IN THE PATH

Columbus wanted to arrive to Asia crossing the Atlantic, but in the middle of the path he found an obstacle: America. They thought that they had arrived to Asia and called the conquered lands "The Indies", later they saw that it was an unknown continent in the West and they called it "The New World".

Atlantic Ocean

Aztecs

Mayans

Pacific Ocean

Incas

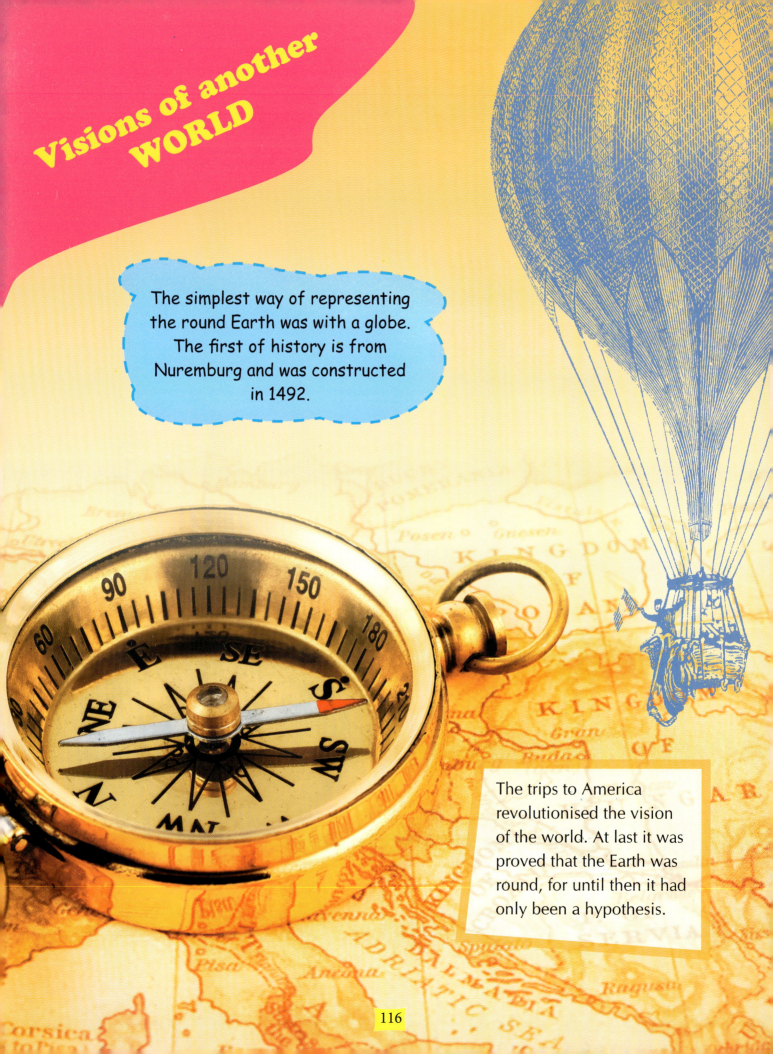

Visions of another WORLD

The simplest way of representing the round Earth was with a globe. The first of history is from Nuremburg and was constructed in 1492.

The trips to America revolutionised the vision of the world. At last it was proved that the Earth was round, for until then it had only been a hypothesis.

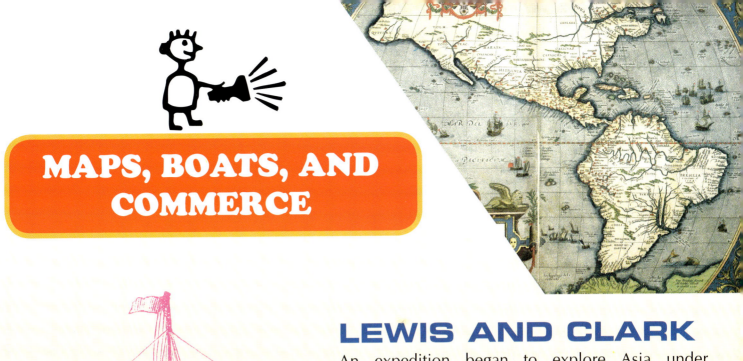

MAPS, BOATS, AND COMMERCE

LEWIS AND CLARK

An expedition began to explore Asia under Meriwether Lewis and William Clark, commissioned by President Jefferson of United States in 1804 - one of their goals were to study the flora and fauna and discovering methods to exploit it economically.

As the commercial routes for Asia were monopolised, the Portuguese and the Spanish looked for alternative routings through the ocean, which improved maps of the world.

The trips to America were possible thanks to the advances in cartography and in navigation.

FROM PORT TO PORT

The portolan charts are the predecessors of modern maps. They were used for navigation, that's why only the coastlines were detailed and black lines crossed the charts joining the ports of arrival and departure.

Did you know that...

The oldest surviving maps are from Mesopotamia made on clay tablets and those from ancient Mediterranean cultures made on mosaic tiles.

America and Américo

America is called so because a cartographer wrote in a map this name to refer to the New World. The name is in honour of Américo Vespucio, who said that Columbus had arrived to a new continent and not to Asia.

21st October 1492
- Columbus and shipmate spot land.
4th January 1493
- He returned to Spain.
25th September 1493
- He went on a second voyage.
30th May 1498
- He sets forth on a third voyage
9th May 1502
- He went on his last voyage.

ATLAS. . .
The first modern atlas had 70 maps. It was called the Theatre of the World and in it the New World already appeared, in the 16th century.

ALIGNMENT OF THE SUN, OF THE POLAR STAR, AND OF THE SOUTHERN CROSS

Jacob's staff

These celestial points were guides for ocean navigation. Thanks to a series of rules for the observation of the stars and of the Sun, the sailors managed to know their latitude, determine local time, etc. One of the instruments was called the Astrolabe.

Determining the geographical length was more complex than the latitude, but one of the forms of measurement was the observation of the Eclipses of the Moon.

MEASURING THE LATITUDE

Another instruments that the sailors used to measure their latitude was Jacob's Staff. With it they calculated the height of the polar star and determined latitude.

WHAT ARE YOUR COORDINATES?

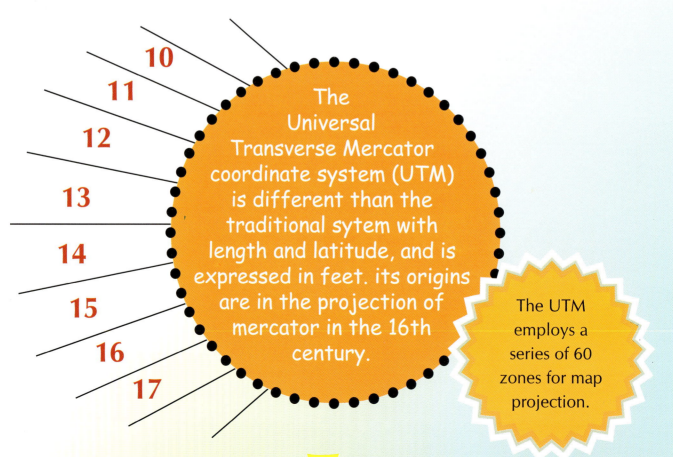

10

11

12

13

14

15

16

17

The Universal Transverse Mercator coordinate system (UTM) is different than the traditional sytem with length and latitude, and is expressed in feet. its origins are in the projection of mercator in the 16th century.

The UTM employs a series of 60 zones for map projection.

1. Locate in the map the country in which you live.

2. If it is above the Equator it will be in the Northern latitude and, if it is below, it is in the Southern latitude. Use the magnifying glass or lupa to look at the value of the nearest horizontal line, which is called a parallel. Like this you will obtain the value in degrees of latitude. For example, 20° parallel to the South.

3. Look for the value of the meridian with the magnifying glass, which is the nearest vertical line. If it is to the right of the 0° Meridian that passes through Greenwich (London) it will be to the East and if it is to the left, it will be to the West.

Material:
• **Lupa**

Now you can play by giving coordinates to any point in the world!

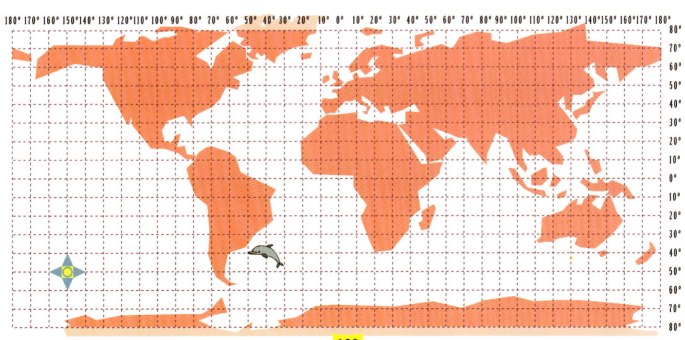

The Mayan civilisation was one of the first in discovering the number zero. The symbol that they used had the form of a conch shell.

Many pre-hispanic civilisations counted with a numbering system of base 20, while at present we use a system of base 10. To say the number 41 they said "one in the third group".

To count and calculate, the Incas used a sort of abacus called yupana, made of stone or mud and with several boxes where stones or grains of corn were placed.

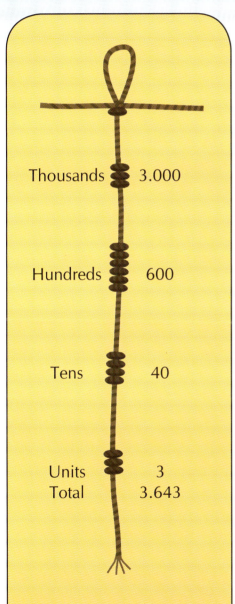

Thousands	3.000
Hundreds	600
Tens	40
Units	3
Total	3.643

THE QUIPO IS A ROPE WITH KNOTS THAT THE INCAS USED TO COUNT WITH

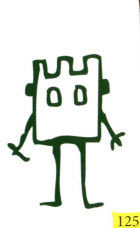

THE MOUNTAIN THAT SMOKES

Popocatepetl is a volcano situated in Mexico that in pre-Hispanic times was worshipped and considered as a God. At present they call it Don Goyo and people perform rites asking for rain for the crops and protection from hail.

Mt. Popocatepetl was the origin of a mudflow that buried the mammoth bones 10,000 years ago. The site was discovered in 1996.

The Spanish climbed the volcano in order to get sulphur to make gunpowder.

Explosive Volcanoes

There are more explosive volcanoes and other calmer ones. The first release gases, spewing lava and pieces of rock with a lot of force, whereas the calmest expel only oozing lava. The explosive volcanoes are usually near the limits of the tectonic plates.

Engineers

The Incas placed great importance on communication and to agriculture. They built important paths, systems of irrigation, and terraces to be able to farm in the mountainous areas.

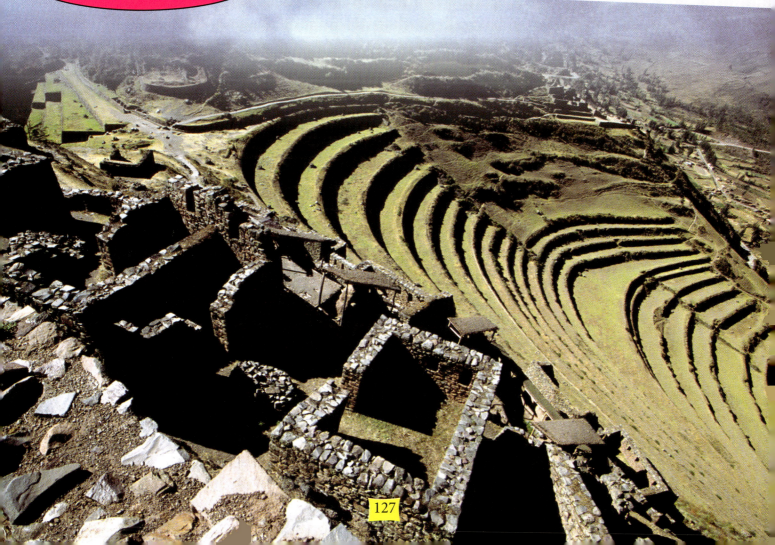

Cocoa was so valuable that it was used as a currency to buy and sell.

BITTER CHOCOLATE

The Mayans and the Mexicans made a drink with cocoa called xocolatl that is totally different to the chocolate that we eat for our afternoon snack. Back then, besides being bitter, it was spicy. Kings, noblemen and soldiers drank it and the doctors recommended it as a stimulant and painkiller.

THE PRE-HISPANIC AMERICAN SOCCER CUP

It seems that the game of the ball that they played in the pre-Colombian America is the predecessor of our current soccer. People played with a ball of rubber in a field shaped like an "I". It was a ritual game related with their vision of the origin of the Universe.

AS MANY SUNS AS WORLDS

According to the Aztecs, four 'Suns' had been created in four previous ages and all died at the end of each era. The fifth Sun was called 'Tonatiuh' and the present era is still his.

Huitzilopochtli, meaning, 'Blue Hummingbird on the left, was the Aztec Sun God.

CROPS OF AMERICA

The corn, the potato, the red pepper and vanilla were cultivated and improved genetically by the peasants of the pre-Hispanic civilisations for centuries before the crop started growing in Europe.

POTATO

CORN

VANILLA

RED PEPPER

AMERICAN COFFEE OR AFRICAN?

The famous coffees of Colombia, Brazil, and Mexico owe their success to Africa, for the coffee plant is of Ethiopian origin.

THE MAGNIFYING GLASS IN THE BOOKS OF SECRETS

These Renaissance books describe recipes of medicine or beauty and marvels of nature. In one of them, it describes the power of the convex lenses to magnify objects, exactly what a magnifying glass or a pair of glasses do.

OBSERVATORIES AND SNAKES

The pre-hispanic cultures had astronomical observatories. One of the best known is The Snail where every solstice, because of an optical effect, the shadow of a snake appears and slithers down the stairs.

Science kept moving away from art and philosophy in the 16th century. The scientists felt the need to create a method to answer questions, so they created the scientific method based on exact calculations, experiments, and repetitions.

Outline of the Scientific Method

1. Observe:

Here your curiosity comes into action!
To observe the world where you live is the first step for a great discovery (or even for answering a simple question).

2 Ask questions:

"How? Where? Why?" There is no wrong question. Release your desire to know and question the world.

3 Make a hypothesis:

It is a possible solution or answer to your question that is based on what you know of the subject.

4 Experiment:

You need to prove your hypothesis. Measure time, weight, length, and compare afterwards.

5 Conclusions:

It is the result of your work. You can confirm your hypothesis, but if it was wrong do not be discouraged, because it is the moment for creating another question and starting again.

Put your creativity into practice! Are you already curious about something or still not yet? Now is the moment! Try and use the stages of the method. You can also be a scientist, even if you do not wear a white coat and are not in a laboratory.

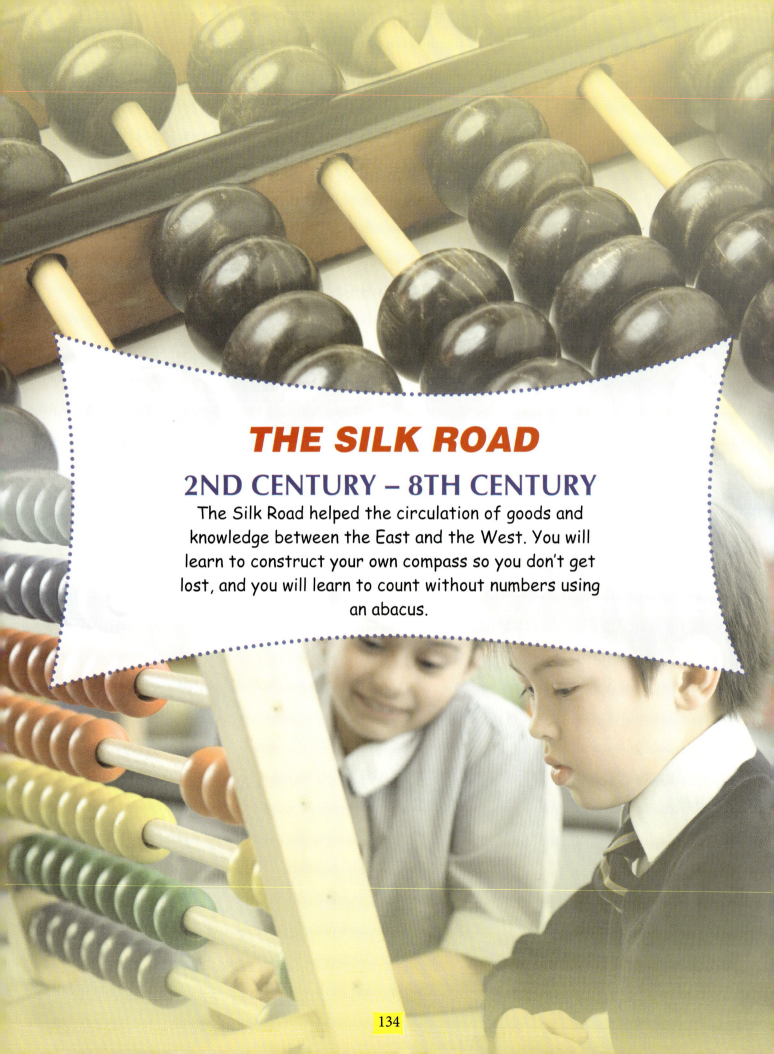

THE SILK ROAD

2ND CENTURY – 8TH CENTURY

The Silk Road helped the circulation of goods and knowledge between the East and the West. You will learn to construct your own compass so you don't get lost, and you will learn to count without numbers using an abacus.

THE SILK ROAD

For almost twelve centuries, the Silk Road was a commercial channel between Asia, Africa, and Europe. The route began for military uses, but it was converted with time into a pathway where very delicate products arrived to the West, such as silk, porcelain or tea, inventions like the compass, and an infinite supply of artistic and scientific knowledge.

The Secret of the Worms

One of the better-kept secrets in former China was the production of a bright and soft fabric: silk. These fabrics crossed thousands of miles along the commercial route that joined the East and the West, called the Silk Road. The secret was in the breeding of silkworms, which made their cocoons with this fine, bright and resistant thread.

From a cocoon of silk we can draw out more than 3,000 feet of continuous filament thread!

The Earth is like a MAGNET

The Earth has a big magnet in its interior that makes other magnets orient to the north and the south. Magnets can be natural, like magnetite, which is a mineral of iron, or artificial magnets, which are materials with iron that magnetise.

ONE OF THE FIRST COMPASSES WAS A FISH BUILT WITH A FINE SHEET OF IRON MAGNETISED SO THAT WHEN FLOATING IN THE WATER IT INDICATED THE NORTH AND THE SOUTH.

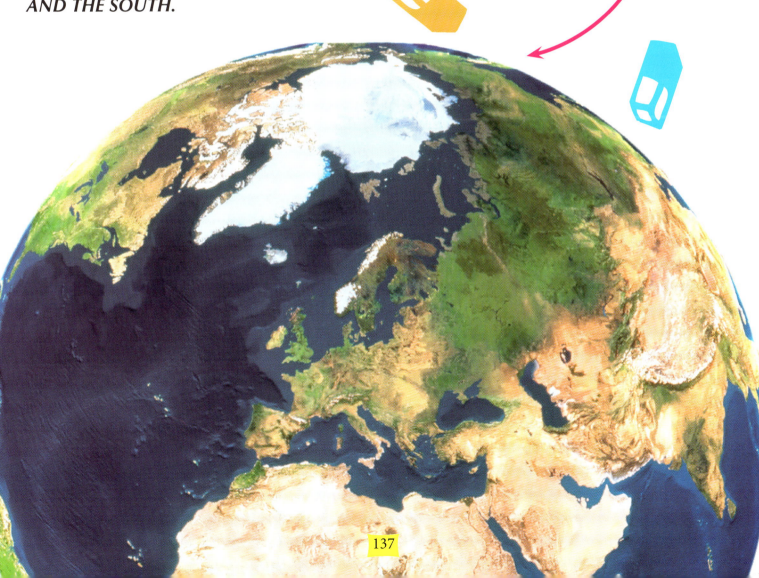

Do not lose the North!

Compasses point to the north thanks to the fact that they have a magnet shaped as an arrow in the needle. About 4,000 years ago the Chinese discovered that the spoons made of magnetite that they used for orienting, moved and pointed towards the south.

Do ants need a compass?

Ants and bees do not need a compass to find their way. In their abdomen and their head they have magnetite with which they orient themselves in their migrations and dances.

Did you know that...

The direction of the North Pole does not coincide exactly with the magnetic north. This fact was known in China 700 years befor it was in the West and it is at present known as magnetic declination.

Earthquakes

Earthquakes are vibrations of the Earth that release a great quantity of energy in a very short time in the form of shock waves. They take place when two tectonic plates rub up against each other. The energy is transmitted from the origin of the seismic wave in the interior of the Earth, called the focus or hypocentre, towards the surface. The point that is right on the focus on the terrestrial surface is called the epicentre.

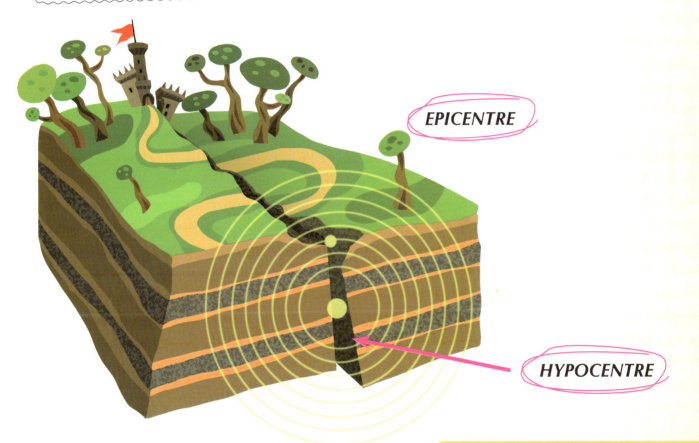

EPICENTRE

HYPOCENTRE

In the 2nd century, the Chinese scientist, Chang Heng invented a curious artifact called the seismoscope, which was used for detecting earthquakes and knowing the direction of the waves. It consists of a vessel of bronze with a pendulum in its interior that moves when there is an earthquake.

EARTHQUAKES, TOADS AND CHINESE DRAGONS

The mechanism made the mouth of a dragon open. Then, the ball of copper that was in its interior fell in the mouth of a toad creating a sound.

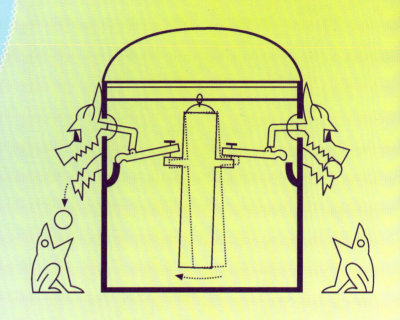

HARVEST OF GINGER AND COPPER

The Chinese knew that if we excavate the ground where ginger grows we can find beds of copper or tin.

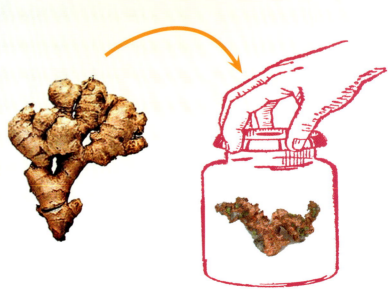

Imaginary interview with...
Shen Kuo
(1031 - 1095 B.C.)

The first instrument to measure air humidity, called a hygrometer, was invented in China in the 2nd century B.C.

- Honourable Shen Kuo, tell us what is your profession?
Yes, of course, I am only a geologist, astronomer, cartographer, weather forecaster, mathematician, engineer, chemist and pharmacologist. But because I have extra time, I am also dedicated to the matters of state of the dynasty of Song, as an ambassador and military general.

- You state that the mountain Taihang in the past was on the coast. Why do you believe that?
Walking through the mountain, I found in the rocks marks of shells. Then I thought that those shells had already been on the coast and that, therefore, the rocks were formed near the sea and in the past. Later, the rocks ascended forming this beautiful mountain.

-Thank you very much. By the way I have to go towards the north of the country, can you tell me the way?
Yes, of course, take this compass and a map, although you have to notice that the north of the compass does not coincide with the north in the map you have. After doing several experiments, I have discovered this problem, but nobody knows it yet.

TRIP TO THE CENTRE OF THE EARTH

Even though we have landed on distant planets, we have not managed to penetrate the Earth more than 8 miles. With the study of shock waves we know that the interior of the Earth has different material and different parts. That's why we divide up the interior of the Earth into layers:

* **CRUST:** Varied solid rocks with some melted parts.
* **MANTLE:** Rocks of silicates in semiliquid state.
* **OUTER CORE:** Liquid iron.
* **INNER CORE:** Iron with a little nickel in solid state.

CRUST

MANTLE

OUTER CORE

INNER CORE

The magnetic poles of the Earth are inverted after a certain number of years. The last inversion happened **740,000** years ago.

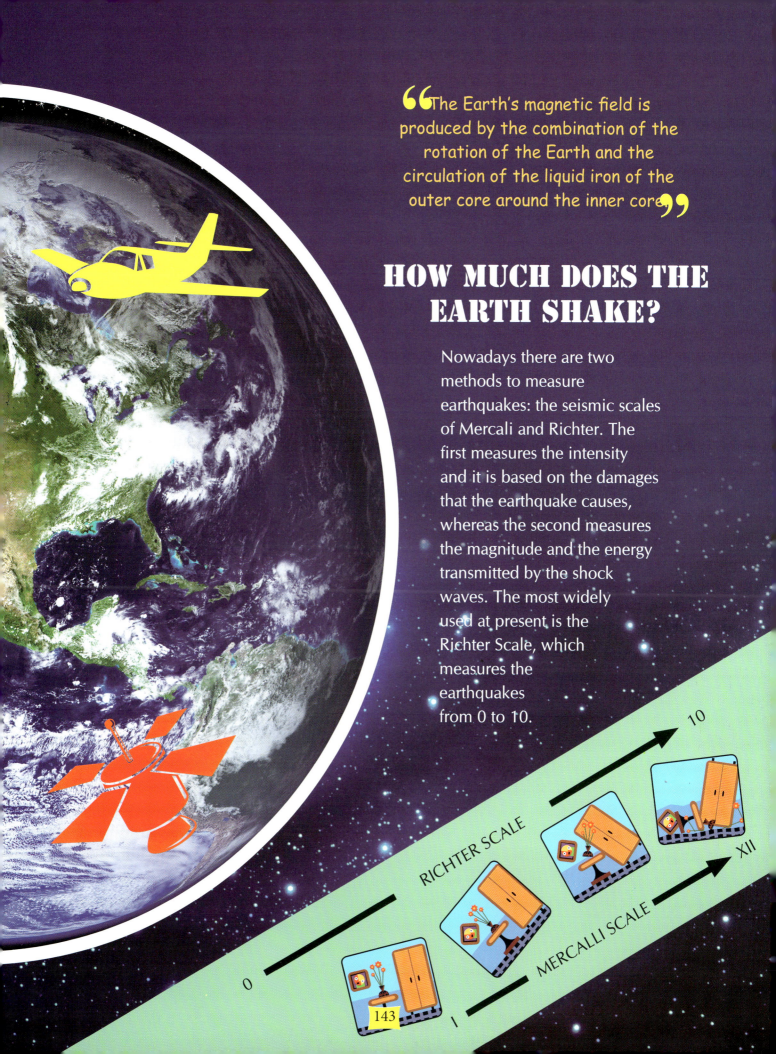

> "The Earth's magnetic field is produced by the combination of the rotation of the Earth and the circulation of the liquid iron of the outer core around the inner core"

HOW MUCH DOES THE EARTH SHAKE?

Nowadays there are two methods to measure earthquakes: the seismic scales of Mercali and Richter. The first measures the intensity and it is based on the damages that the earthquake causes, whereas the second measures the magnitude and the energy transmitted by the shock waves. The most widely used at present is the Richter Scale, which measures the earthquakes from 0 to 10.

RICHTER SCALE

MERCALLI SCALE

0

10

I

XII

CAN YOU IMAGINE COUNTING WITHOUT NUMBERS?

When there were no written numbers yet, people counted with the fingers of their hands and their feet.

SELLING AND COUNTING

Until numbers were invented, in businesses the abacus was used. This is a very old instrument of calculation used especially by Eastern cultures.

Even today, in Asia they teach the abacus at school and use it in many stores.

Today, calculation competitions with the abacus are celebrated in Japan. On some occasions abacists are confronted against competitors with calculators. And most of the times the abacists are faster!

ABACUSES AGAINST CALCULATORS

Adding and Subtracting with the **abacus**

The abacus is formed by a series of beads that are attached to rods. The beads of the lower part are worth 1 and those of the top are worth 5. The beads move up or down so only the ones that are up are counted. Besides, each of the columns also has a different value. On the right are the singles and in the following column are the tens and so on.

To form a number the beads of value 1 go up, and if the number is greater than five, we move a bead of 5 too.

For example, the number 173 will be represented by: 3 beads of value 1 in the column of the units 2 beads of value 1 and 1 bead of value 5 in the column of the tens (2 + 5 = 7) and 1 bead of value 1 in the column of the hundreds.

The Koreans and Japanese imported the abacus from China in 1400 CE and 1600 CE.

The Chinese call the abacus, Suan Pan (Suan means calculating)

With the abacus you can do several mathematical operations, such as addition and subtraction. The first figure that you want to add or subtract is represented in the abacus. To add, you add the beads of the second figure, but if you want to subtract you have to remove the beads.

YOU BELONG TO THE COSMOS

The Chinese way of understanding life is tied up with energy and with the human being as inseparable parts of Nature and of the Universe. The Chinese traditional medicine is based on the Tao; its components are the Yin and the Yang, two elements of opposed and complementary forces, present in everything, and that coexist, in a harmonic balance in healthy people. When this balance breaks, illness forms.

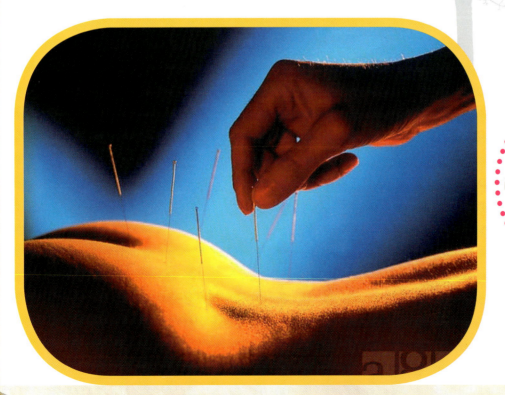

Chinese medicine uses plants, but it also uses compounds of mineral and animal origin.

A long hike to the West

Chinese medicine has about 3,000 years of history. The oldest book that is known is of the 5th century before Christ. It describes the Yin and the Yang, it talks about the organs, viscera, the meridians, of the Qì (vital energy), of the circulation of the blood, the causes of the illnesses, the methods to diagnose, the points of acupuncture and the methods to insert the needles.

Prick me, it hurts!

In the 17th century, Jesuit missionaries returned from China saying that illnesses could heal from the punctures of needles in certain points of the body. This way of curing is known as acupuncture, and it prevents and treats illnesses acting at points of energy and blending the body with the mind. At present it is used to cure several illnesses in human beings and also in animals.

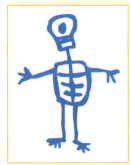

EXPERIMENT

Natural Medicine

Mix 1 ounce of essence of rosemary with four cups of olive oil. This oil of rosemary can be used to rub and massage the skin. The curative properties of this plant decrease muscular and rheumatic pains.

Curative cigar?

There is a cigar that is used in Eastern medicine, called "moxa", which does not have anything to do with the tobacco that is usually smoked. It is made with leaves of artemisia and burns near the skin to improve health.

Chinese medicine uses plants, but it also uses compounds of mineral and animal origin.

CURIOSITIES

The plant of tea, with which green tea and black tea is made, is one of the 50 basic herbs of Chinese traditional medicine.

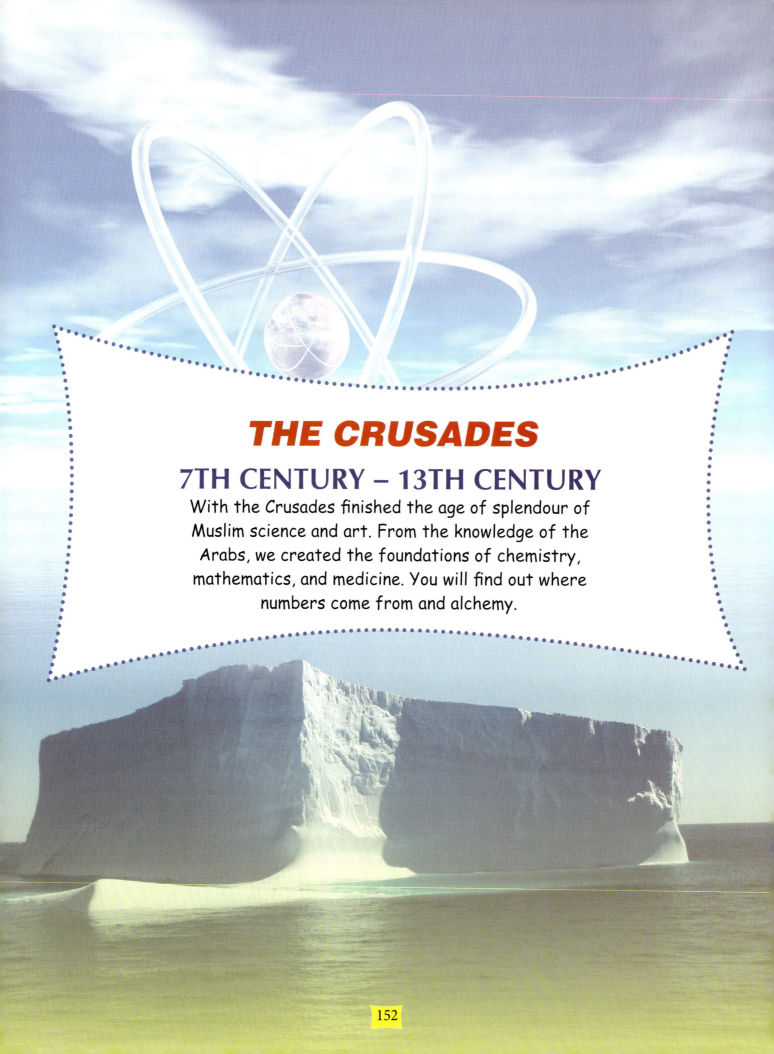

THE CRUSADES

7TH CENTURY – 13TH CENTURY

With the Crusades finished the age of splendour of Muslim science and art. From the knowledge of the Arabs, we created the foundations of chemistry, mathematics, and medicine. You will find out where numbers come from and alchemy.

THE CRUSADES

 7th century – 13th century (From Mohammed till the end of the Crusades)

"Look for knowledge, even if you have to travel to China." (Mohammed)

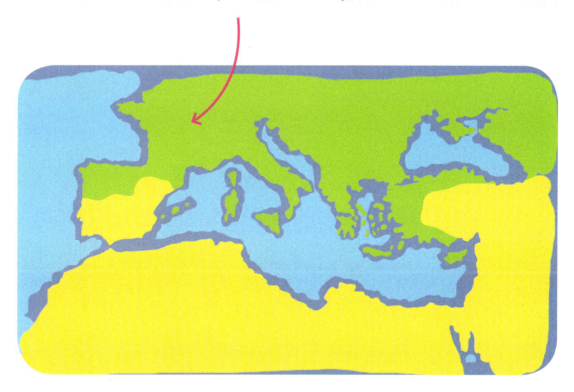

The Crusades are the wars during which the Christians expelled the Arabs from Europe and the Middle East. With the wars came the end of the period of splendour of the sciences and of Muslim art. The Arabs incorporated knowledge from Greece, India, and China to their science, and made their own contributions to the development of astronomy, chemistry, mathematics, medicine, and biology.

What time is it?

The Arab sundials were plates of marble or of copper with a needle in the centre. According to the shadow that it cast the hour of the day could be read. To be able to orient, the direction of the Mecca was marked on the plate.

The expansion of Arab culture and science took place from the time of Mohammed who united all the tribes of the peninsula of Arabia under the religion of the Islam.

THE ALCHEMISTS

The alchemists knew the techniques of transforming some materials into others, and to make miraculous remedies, poisons, and magical potions. The Egyptians, Greek, Hindus and Chinese used these techniques for centuries, but they were named after the Arabs: "Alchemy", which in Arabic means "the art", since for them it was one of the most important kinds of wisdom. Alchemy is the origin of chemistry and of pharmacy.

The Magnum Opus! It is an alchemical term - process of creating the Philosopher's Stone. Personal and spiritual transmutation had, hypothetically, four phases:

- Nigredo: blackening or putrefaction;
- Albedo: whitening or washing away of impurities;
- Citrinitas: yellowing or transmutation into silver or gold;
- Rubedo: reddening or assumed colour of Philosopher's Stone.

ANY METAL COULD BE GOLD!

The alchemists passed centuries looking for two potions:

THE PHILOSOPHER'S STONE: for transforming metals into gold.

THE ELIXIR OF LIFE: to extend life to immortality. They did not find either of the two, but in their search they discovered new materials and new methods for transforming them.

THE GREEK FIRE

With a mixture of quicklime, oil and sulphur, a Syrian alchemist saved Constantinople from Muslim attack. When in contact with water, the quicklime caught fire and the oil burned ablaze! The Muslims ran away impressed.

Imaginary Interview with...
MARIE ANNE LAVOISIER
Mother of Modern Chemistry
(1758-1836)

Mrs. Lavoisier, what is your profession?
I am a chemist, and I work with my husband Antoine in a laboratory.

-Chemistry, that's interesting! Could you explain to us what exactly chemistry is?
For my husband and me, Alchemy has remained oldfashioned. That gang of crazy people who searched for mysterious remedies are falling behind. Chemistry is different; the laws are logical as in the other sciences.

-Which laws are those?
At the moment we have only proven one: that "mass is neither created nor is it destroyed, it only changes". But I am sure very soon many other laws will be discovered.

What is an atom?

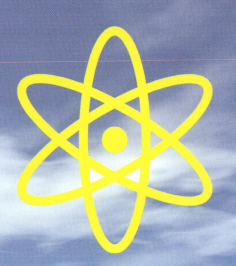

The protons attract the electrons, but if the electrons approach the nucleus, they are repelled.

Finally the electrons remain floating around the nucleus giving a stable structure to the atom.

The atoms are formed by three types of particles:

PROTONS:
They have positive charges and are in the nucleus.

NEUTRONS:
They do not have a charge, that's why they are neutral.
They are also in the nucleus.

ELECTRONS:
They have a negative charge and move around the nucleus.

We have to name the elements!

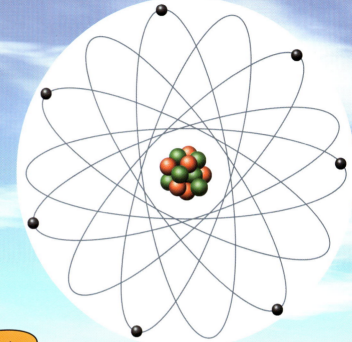

The chemists soon realised that they needed a language to be able to express the formulas of the chemical reactions. They started to represent each of the chemical elements with letters. These are some examples:

OXYGEN: O

Sodium: Na

Chlorine: Cl

Carbon: C

Hydrogen: H

ELECTRONS (CHARGE-)

PROTONS (CHARGE+)

NEUTRONS (NO CHARGE)

Together as friends

Each one of the elements is joined to other elements forming molecules. But they are not joined with all of them, only with those that are compatible, in the same way that we join with our friends.

The molecules are, therefore, the union of several atoms. These are some examples:

Water: H2O
(two atoms of hydrogen and one of oxygen)

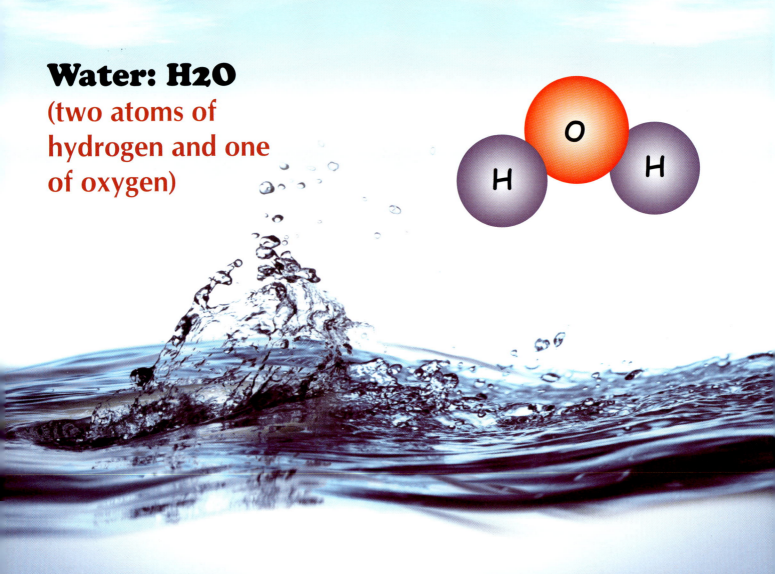

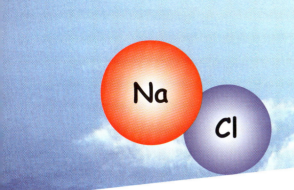

Salt: Na Cl

One atom of sodium (Na) and another of Chlorine (Cl)

TASTY OR POISONOUS?

Curiously, the formula of salt is very similar to that of bleach. Only an atom of oxygen marks the difference between tasty or poisonous food.

Bleach: Na Cl O

Salt: Na Cl

The House of Wisdom was a university in Baghdad where different areas of knowledge were studied.

Ice, water, and steam are all water

Did you know that...

Water is one of the few substances that become bigger when it is solid?

Yes, the solids normally occupy less space than the liquids, which take up less space than the gases. However, not with water. If you put it in a container with water in the freezer and leave it for some hours, when taking it out you will see that the ice has grown. This happens because the structure of the ice leaves very big spaces among the atoms.

Distillation

Distillation is a method that is used to separate two mixed substances. In the process both substances are transformed into gas at different temperatures. The mixture warms up until the first substance starts to vapourise and, when this finishes, we stop warming it up and we cool the gas so that it transforms again into liquid.

THE DISTILLING
DEVICE IS CALLED
AN ALEMBIC

The Arabs used many chemical reactions for the extraction of substances and the preparation of medicines. These products were marketed in many countries, from Europe to Asia, thanks to the Muslim expansion.

Milk with sugar

When we put sugar in the milk it dissolves, but, if we keep on putting sugar, there will be a point when it will not dissolve and it will sink to the bottom. This is called precipitation.

Distillation also occurs in nature. For example: the sea water is salty, but when it evaporates only the water evaporates.

Experiment of
PRECIPITATION:

Material:
- *Milk*
- *Vinegar or lemon*
- *Paper filter (for coffee) or a rag or a handkerchief*

We are going to see how, when putting milk in contact with different acids, precipitation takes place.

- Put a little milk in a glass with some drops of vinegar or of lemon.

- Observe what happens and let it settle a while. What do you observe?

- You can separate the solid from the liquid with a filter, a rag or a handkerchief. How is the solid obtained?

You can also see the reaction of milk with tonic, a cola drink, or juices.

"There are only two sciences: **THEOLOGY** (salvation of the soul) and **MEDICINE** (salvation of the body)"

Since Mohammed said these words, the Muslims started to show interest in medicine, basing their studies on Greek medicine. The books written by Rhazes and Avicena spread their knowledge through the entire world. In them they talk about every illness, analyse its symptoms and suggest possible treatment.

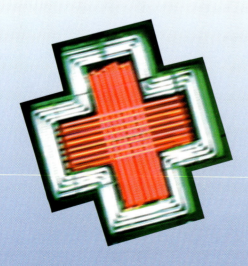

From alchemy, the **pharmacy** is born

The first experiences of alchemy used fire to transform matter: from mineral to iron, from sand to glass... With time new chemical reactions were discovered that created remedies like alcohol or plaster. These substances revolutionised medicine.

Stories that cure

In the book 'One Thousand and One Nights', the character Scheherazade relates detailed stories on passions and illnesses that were read in the hospitals as part of the treatment of the sick.

The Arab numbers travelled from
India

The numbers that we use at present, from 0 to 9, come from India, but are usually called "Arab numbers" because it was the Arabs who brought them to the West.

Did you know that...

The Arabs translated Greek mathematics and Hindu astronomy into Arabic and created big mathematical schools. The most important were those of Cordova, Seville and Granada.

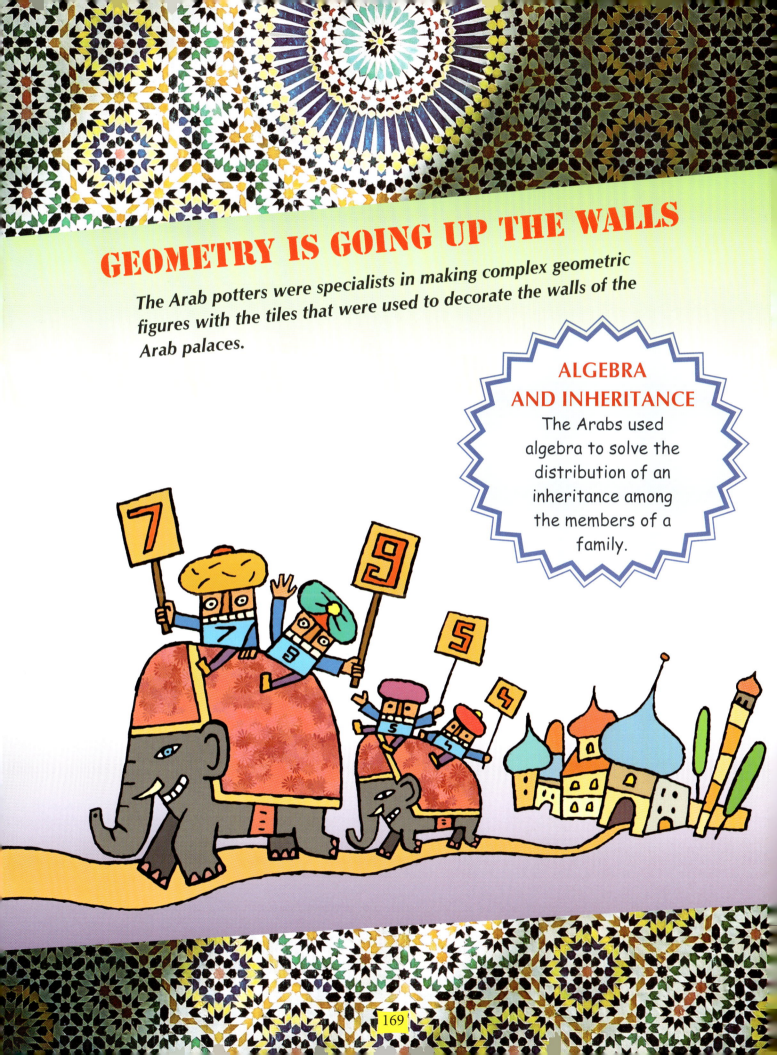

GEOMETRY IS GOING UP THE WALLS

The Arab potters were specialists in making complex geometric figures with the tiles that were used to decorate the walls of the Arab palaces.

ALGEBRA AND INHERITANCE

The Arabs used algebra to solve the distribution of an inheritance among the members of a family.

Imaginary Interview with
LEONARDO FIBONACCI
(1170-1250)

Interview with Leonardo of Pisa, also known as "Fibonacci".

-Mr. Fibonacci, you say that you have discovered a new system of calculation?
-They are the Arabic numbers, but, in fact, I am not the one who has discovered them. The Arabs have already been using them for five centuries and even they learned them from the Hindus.

- What is revolutionary about this new system?
-It is much more effective than the Roman numerals at calculating; doing addition or subtraction is much easier and faster. Besides it adds a very special number that is 0, for, although at first sight it has no value, it is capable of changing the value of the other numbers according to its position.

- To finish, could you prove us the advantages by doing the same calculation in Roman numerals and in Arab numbers?

For example 365 + 437.
-I would like to do it in both systems, but I do not have either the paper or the time to make it with Roman numerals. I will make it with Arabic numbers:

$$
\begin{array}{r}
365 \\
+437 \\
\hline
802
\end{array}
$$

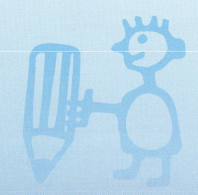

Paper for writing

The first papers in China were of silk and bamboo. As they were of low quality, they were used mainly to wrap. To write they used wooden small boards and cloths of silk, but paper started to be used with time because it was easier to store and to transport.

PAPER TO SPREAD IDEAS

The Arabs learned to create paper from the Chinese and went on to start using other materials, such as linen or hemp. In these papers they wrote the translations of Greek works and their own knowledge, spreading it all through their empire.

Arrival to Europe

After conquering the Iberian Peninsula, the Arabs did not waste their time and established their first workshop of paper production. Al-Andalus, as they called Spain, was the centre of teaching medicine and mathematics.

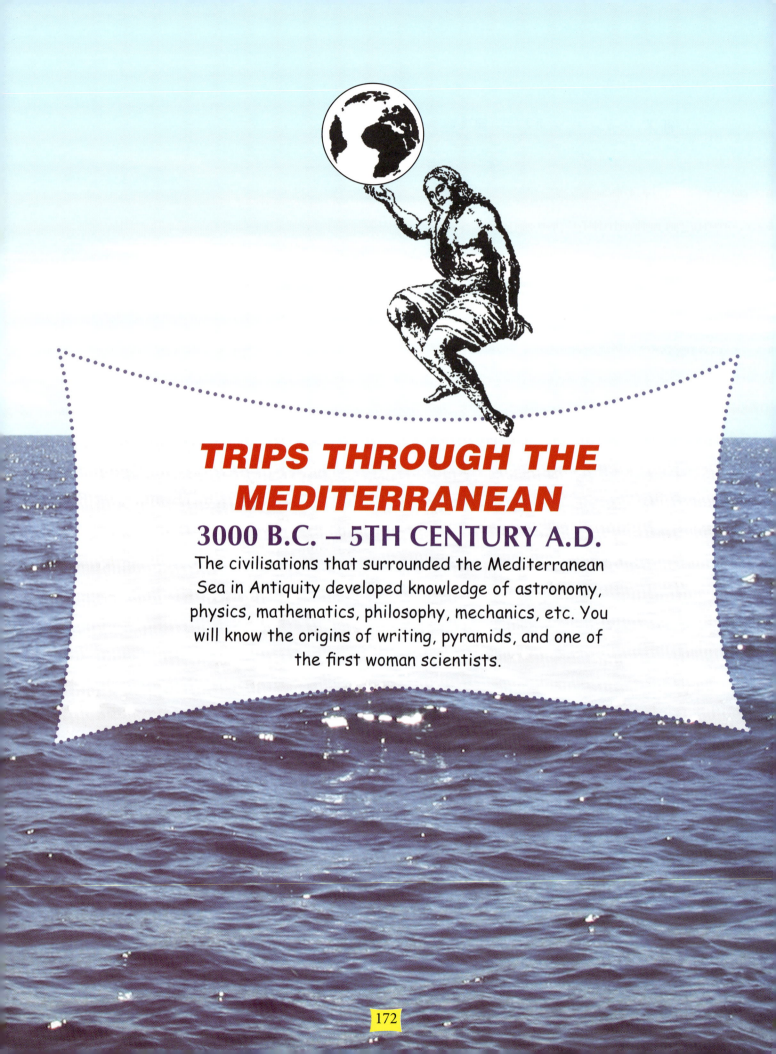

TRIPS THROUGH THE MEDITERRANEAN

3000 B.C. – 5TH CENTURY A.D.

The civilisations that surrounded the Mediterranean Sea in Antiquity developed knowledge of astronomy, physics, mathematics, philosophy, mechanics, etc. You will know the origins of writing, pyramids, and one of the first woman scientists.

THE CAPITAL OF KNOWLEDGE

Alexandria had the oldest library and a museum that was like a university in which all the great wise men of the age taught and did research.

The Mediterranean Sea has always been a place where cultures cross. The traders took their merchandise from port to port and in turn spread knowledge. Also the expansion of the Greek empire into Egypt, Mesopotamia and the East brought knowledge of other people.

Italy

Greece

Caspian Sea

Mediterranean see

Sumer (Ancient Mesopotamia)

Egypt

Red Sea

"Give me a place to stand on, and I will move the Earth."

(Archimedes)

HAS THE SUN HIDDEN BEHIND THE MOON?

When we see them from the Earth, the Sun and the Moon have the same size approximately. However, the Sun is 400 times bigger, but it is 400 times further than the Moon. This makes total eclipses of the Sun possible.

PRECISE ECLIPSES

According to the calculation carried out by the astronomers of Mesopotamia, the movements of the Sun and the Moon are repeated every 18 years. Thanks to this calculation, called cycle of Saros, the lunar and solar eclipses can be predicted from thousands of years ago.

LEGENDS IN THE DARKNESS

All the civilisations have looked towards the stars to be able to orient themselves in the darkness, to measure time, and to tell the legends of their people. To improve their understanding, they grouped together the stars in imaginary drawings, called constellations, which represented characters or elements of their mythology.

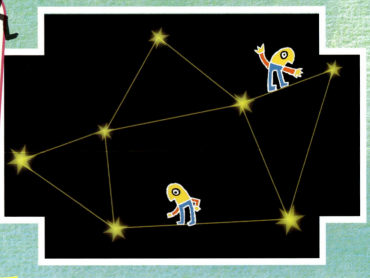

WHICH SIGN ARE YOU?

The Sumerians divided up the stars that are in the strip of sky where the Sun and the planets pass into twelve constellations that compose the signs of the zodiac. According to astrology we are the sign of the zodiac that is covered up by the Sun on the day of our birth.

Sagitarius

AND AT NIGHT, HOW DO YOU TELL TIME?

The clepsydras are clocks of water that were used at night or inside buildings, where the sundials did not have any use. The ancient Egyptians used them, afterwards the Greeks and later the Romans. They consisted of several containers in which drop by drop the water passed through a container to another and like this they could calculate the time.

EGYPT,
THE CRADLE OF WRITING

About 5,000 years ago the Egyptians started to record hieroglyphs in wood or stone. In them they represented scenes of daily life, animals, plants, parts of the body, etc. These drawings that decorated temples, pyramids, and objects are the beginnings of writing.

The importance of the scribes

In ancient Egypt, only a few knew how to write and they were called scribes. They were put in charge of counting the foods, to write down the level of the Nile, or to document the number of slaves used in the construction of temples and pyramids.

Writing in mud

As the Sumerians did not know how to make papyri of quality, they started to write the language they spoke on mud, on plates, cylinders, or prisms. Their writing is named cuneiform..

Did you know that...

Up to the discovery of the Rosetta Stone in 1799 the hieroglyphs could not be deciphered?

Imaginary Interview with Eratosthenes

(around 275 - 195 B.C.)

-Mr. Eratosthenes, you say that the Earth has 24,615 miles of diameter. Could you tell us how you calculated it?

The papyri of the library of Alexandria say that in the city of Sienna, on the 21st of June at midday, the homes do not have shadow because the Sun appears in the sky as high as possible. However, the same day at the same hour, in the city of Alexandria, the objects do have a shadow.

-So what?

-It occurred to me to measure the angle that those shadows form and I sent a regiment of soldiers to measure the steps that there were between both cities.

-Good, and to what does all this come?

-With that data and my knowledge of trigonometry I started to calculate the size of the Earth and this result came out. But that is not everything: I have also calculated the distance between the Earth and the Sun, and the Earth and the Moon.

IMAGINE THAT YOU DO NOT HAVE SUFFICIENT FORCE TO MOVE SOMETHING...

In order to multiply our force, we can use several inventions. These inventions has been known from more than 2,000 years ago.

The Greeks proved their knowledge of physics by inventing, building, and using every type of gadget.

How are the PYRAMIDS built?

TO BUILD THE PYRAMIDS, THE EGYPTIANS USED THE "INCLINED PLANE" THAT ALLOWS YOU TO RAISE WEIGHT WITH LESS EFFORT. THEY MADE RAMPS WITH SAND, ON WHICH THEY RAISED THE STONES AND THEN TOOK AWAY THE SAND AFTERWARDS.

It is said that Archimedes invented the "compound pulley" around 200 B.C. and was capable of lifting a ship and raising it to the coast.

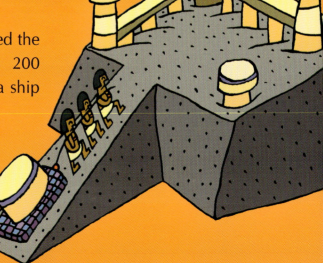

Wheels with teeth

THE GEARS ARE COMBINATIONS OF COGS. ANTIKYTHERA, THE OLDEST KNOWN MECHANISM, IS A GREEK CALENDAR THAT INDICATED THE FUTURE POSITIONS OF THE SUN, THE MOON AND THE STARS.

THE OLDEST AND LEAST OLD-FASHIONED INVENTION

The wheel is considered one of the most important inventions of humanity. Of stone, of wood, of metal; and of rubber, wheels have been used through out history. If we put weight on skates, logs, or wheels it is much easier to move it and like this we have a cart.

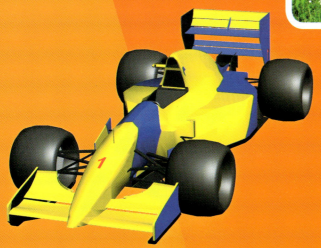

The cars of Formula 1 have little to do with the old cart, but the wheels are still there... Nothing better has been found.

GREEK ART

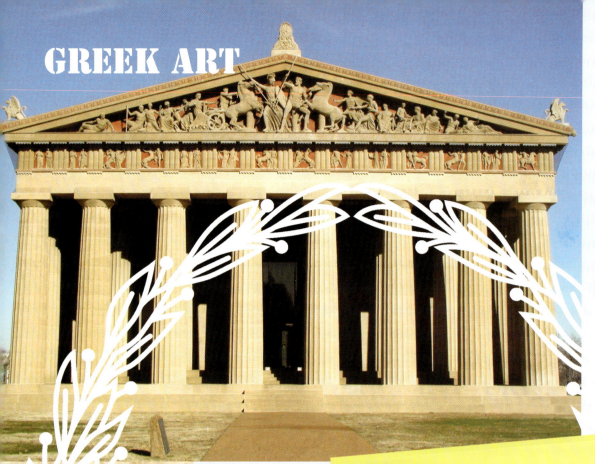

Epicurus founded a school of philosophy in Athens where he developed the search for happiness and the struggle against fears that cause pain (fear of the gods, of death, and of pain and failure).

It's logical!

Aristotle developed rules of logic to apply them in science as well as in philosophy. Science is the result of building complex systems of logical reasoning.

A simple example of logic is:
"All human beings are mortal".
"All Greeks are human".
Therefore, one arrives at the valid conclusion that: "All Greeks are mortal".

Did you know that...

The Greeks called the Romans "builders of sewers, roadways and bridges" because they were not artists: they did not know how to use marble to raise something as sublime as the Parthenon. The Greek art is the human expression of beauty and its harmony with the nature that surrounds us. What the Romans gave to engineering, the Greeks gave to art.

CRYSTAL CLEAR

The history of creating glass can be traced back to 3500 B. C. But only important buildings such as palaces and cathedrals had glass windows, for at that time glass was made only in small quantities and was too expensive for use in everyday buildings.

Did you know that...

The first type of glass used in construction was the stained glass in the windows of palaces and cathedrals.

HYPATIA

of Alexandria
(370?-415?)

-You are considered one of the wisest people of humanity. Could you explain to us why?

It must be because I have developed mathematics and astronomy to a level that was not surpassed for centuries. However, my works were lost when the library of Alexandria disappeared, and that's why very little is known about me today.

-But everyone did not agree with your discoveries, is that true?

Well, I think what they did not agree with was, being a woman scientist and also not religious. The Bishop of Alexandria persecuted me for years with false accusations until her private army killed me.

-It is because of this that you were considered the first victim of religious fanaticism?

Yes, but I am not the only one. Throughout history, female scientists have been almost always persecuted or ignored. The witches, without going further, were connoisseurs of alchemy and medicine, and ended up in the bonfire. Even many of the books written by female scientists have had to be published by men in order to avoid problems.

Experiment
CURVATURE OF THE EARTH:

If you see a ship on the horizon that is moving away from the coast, it gives you the feeling that it sinks, because the things that disappear last are the sails. Based on this effect, Aristotle proved that the Earth is round.

If you glue a little boat on a ball and you observe it while you keep turning the ball, you will understand this phenomenon!

ARMS INSTEAD OF MACHINES

Romans made use of the force of slaves for their constructions, for it was the cheapest energy they had. They did not develop their sources of energy much, but they did have the gadgets to build, such as cranes, pulleys, or scaffolds. Still today many bridges, aqueducts, theatres, and roadways remain standing.

The Roman art was practical: it used concrete and bricks to lift enormous constructions.

THE MILITARY ENGINEERING OF CAESAR

Engineering for military purposes is a science as old as war. Caesar had the best army of the world in his hands and the best engineers of the time.

THE OLDEST ALLOY

There is archaeological evidence that around 3500 B.C. molten copper and tin were being mixed together to produce a metal alloy: bronze. This era is known as the Bronze Age.

Bells, weapons, statues, instruments were made of bronze, an alloy of 78 percent copper and 22 percent tin.

GOLD RUSH

Because of its rarity, gold has been prized as a precious element ever since ancient times; it has been used for coins, jewelry, and objects that represent luxury and power.

BRONZE TO IRON

After Bronze came the Iron Age. It occupies a privileged place in metallurgy because its coming into widespread use represented a revolution in how our species lived.

EXPERIMENT OF THE PRINCIPLE OF
ARCHIMEDES

1. Fill a container of chickpeas, beans, lentils or rice almost to the top.
2. Put the ping-pong ball inside with about one inch of depth in the legumes.
3. Place the ball of steel on the surface.
4. Shake the container softly for a few seconds and you will see how the ball of steel goes inside, while the ping-pong ball appears floating on the surface. This is due to the ball of steel being much heavier than ping-pong ball.
5. You can repeat the experiment putting both balls deep down or leaving both of them in the surface.

MATERIAL:
- A BIG CONTAINER
- CHICKPEAS, BEANS, LENTILS OR RICE (NOT COOKED)
- A BALL OF STEEL OF ABOUT 1 INCH (OR ANOTHER HEAVY OBJECT)
- A PING-PONG BALL

EUREKA, I FOUND IT!

This is what Archimedes said when he discovered his most famous "principle". The king of Syracuse had ordered him to prove whether his crown was of solid gold. It is said that he found the solution when he was taking a bath. If he submerged the crown in the water, the level of water would go up the same as if he introduced an object of pure gold with the same weight as the crown. As the crown was mixed with silver, which is less dense, the level went up less than it would have with solid gold. This way he discovered that they had tricked the king.

SOMETHING TO PROTECT

Since people began to migrate more than thousands of years ago, they needed dwellings to protect themselves and their families. Little by little these dwellings have undergone simple modifications.

Nomads had to depend on shelter offered by the terrain like leaves, branches, hides, cloth, etc.

Others constructed semi-permanent shelters like huts by packing a framework of branches with a mixture of earth and animal dung sticks and skins.

Nothing but blocks of ice are used by Eskimos for constructing their igloos, which protect them against the cold; the interior may be 32°F (0°C), while outside it is minus 25°F(minus 30°C) or colder.

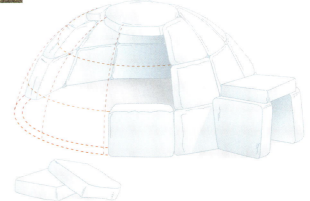

THE FIRST DURABLE MATERIALS

Stone and compressed earth were surely the first durable materials used in construction. This system makes it possible to construct large houses with windows, but it requires very thick walls when beams are used for the roof.

BAKE THE CLAY!

The practice of baking blocks of clay to harden it is very ancient; it was used more than 6,000 years ago in Asia for making bricks. The combined use of bricks and wooden beams made it possible to construct houses of more than a single storey, with several rooms, doors, and windows.

GLOSSARY

ABACUS. Object that is used for carrying out operations of calculation: adding, subtracting, multiplying, etc.

ACTUALISM. It is a principle of Geology according to which the geological processes that acted in the past are the same ones that act in the present.

ALGEBRA. Area of mathematics that studies structures, relations, and quantities.

ASTRONOMICAL OBSERVATORY.
Space dedicated to the observation and study of the sky and the celestial bodies. They are usually in high places and far from big populations.

ATOM. It is the smallest part of a chemical element and cannot be divided into smaller parts through chemical processes.

BACTERIUM. Very small organism composed by only one cell.

BIG BANG. Theory that explains the origin of the Universe with a great explosion.

BIG CRUNCH. Theory that explains the end of the Universe with a great implosion or collapse.

BIODIVERSITY. The variety of animal species and plants that exist on Earth.

CARTOGRAPHY. Scientific area that is about the study and the elaboration of maps.

COMPASS. Instrument that is used for orientating oneself. Its operation is based on the phenomenon of magnetism.

CONSTELLATION. Set of stars that designate an area of the cosmos.

DNA. Abbreviation of desoxyribonucleic acid. It is the hereditary material that contains the instructions for living creatures to function and develop.

DYNAMO. Device that transforms the mechanical energy into electrical energy.

ELECTROMAGNETISM. Study of the electrical and magnetic phenomena.

ENERGY. It is the capacity to carry out work. It is a property that can be observed in its transformations into different types of energy.

FOSSIL. Remains or bones of organisms that lived in the past and that have been preserved.

GALAXY. A group of thousands of stars that turn constantly on an axis.

GEOMETRY. Area of mathematics that focuses on the study of the properties and measurement of space.

GPS. Abbreviation of the Global PositioningSystem. With several satellites and a receiver of waves it manages to determine the position of an object that is in any part of the world.

GRAVITY. Force of attraction among objects. It is the force that the Earth exerts on objects and living creatures that, as a consequence, have a weight.

INTERNET. It is an open media in which any person or entity can send and receive information. It is based on the operation of a network of interconnected computers.

LATITUDE. Distance measured in degrees starting from a point at the Equator.

LONGITUDE. Distance from a point to the meridian of Greenwich.

LUNAR ECLIPSE. Partial vision of the Moon or reddening of it. It happens when the Earth does not let the light of the Sun arrive to theMoon.

MAGNETIC FIELD. Area of the space where there is a magnetic force. The magnets are oriented to this region.

MAP. Graphic representation of a territory that is usually in two dimensions. Can be represented by physical, political, cultural data, etc.

METEORITE. Fragment of rock that originates from space and that falls on the surface of a planet or satellite.

MOLECULE. Particle formed by several equal or different atoms of elements.

MYTHOLOGY. They are fantastic stories told from a religion or culture about their vision of the world and the universe. Some are based on real facts.

NATURAL SELECTION. It is one of the mechanisms of biological evolution in which the organisms better adapted to the environment are those that persist in front of the poorly adapted ones.

PLATE TECTONICS. Theory that explains the shifting of the continents on the tectonic plates, the formation of the chains of mountains, of the volcanoes, and of the earthquakes.

RADIOACTIVITY. Natural phenomenon that consists of the emission of radiations by the nucleus of radioactive chemical elements.

SATELLITE. Object that turns around another. It can be natural, as with the Moon, or artificial, as the satellites of telecommunications.

SHOCK WAVE. Wave provoked by the movements of the Earth's crust that propagates these vibrations across the land producing earthquakes.

SOLAR ECLIPSE. Total or partial darkening of the sky due to the position of the Moon between the Earth and the Sun.

SOURCE OF ENERGY. It is the natural resource and the technology that is used to create energy.

SPECIES. It is a unit of classification of plants and animals that defines a group of organisms capable of reproducing and giving rise to fertile descendants.

TRAIT. A term of genetics about the visible or quantifiable expression of the genes.

X-RAYS. It is a type of electromagnetic radiation. Although prolonged exposure is dangerous it is used a lot in medicine with different applications.

Bibliography

◊ Illustrated story of science of the university of cambridge. Volume i, ii, iii, iv. Colin a. Ronan, jorge zahar editor, río de janeiro, 2oo1. (1983 First edition)

◊ Story of science.
Javier ordóñez, víctor navarro and josé manuel sánchez ron, editor espasa calpe, madrid, 2003.

◊ Story of science.
Michel serres (ed.), Editor cátedra, madrid, 1991. (1989 First edition)

◊ Um olhar sobre o passado: story of science in latin america. Silvia f. De m. Figueroa, editor unicamp, campinas-sp, 2000.

◊ Copain des sciences. Le guide des scientifiques en herbe. Robert pince, milan jeunesse, toulouse, 1998.

Acknowledgements

For silvia fernanda de mendonça figueirôa, professor of history of natural sciences at the universidad estatal de campinas (brasil), for giving us the idea of telling the history of science through trips and for her suggested readings.

Photography credits

© Getty images
© Age fotostock
© Fotolia